Oryx Sourcebook Series in Business and Management

The Global Economy
An Information Sourcebook

Oryx Sourcebook Series in Business and Management

Paul Wasserman, Series Editor

**Oryx Sourcebook Series
in Business and Management**

The Global
Economy
An Information
Sourcebook

by A. M. Abdul Huq
St. John's University (New York) Library

WITHDRAWN

Phoenix • New York
ORYX PRESS
1988

The rare Arabian Oryx is believed to have inspired the myth of the unicorn. This desert antelope became virtually extinct in the early 1960s. At that time several groups of international conservationists arranged to have 9 animals sent to the Phoenix Zoo to be the nucleus of a captive breeding herd. Today the Oryx population is over 800, and over 400 have been returned to reserves in the Middle East.

Copyright © 1988 by
The Oryx Press
2214 North Central at Encanto
Phoenix, AZ 85004-1483

Published simultaneously in Canada

Printed and Bound in the United States of America

∞ The paper used in this publication meets the minimum requirements of American National Standard for Information Science—Permanence of Paper for Printed Library Materials, ANSI Z39.48, 1984.

Library of Congress Cataloging-in-Publication Data

Huq, A. M. Abdul.
    The global economy : an information sourcebook / by A.M. Abdul Huq.
    p. cm. — (Oryx sourcebook series in business and management ; no. 15)
    Includes index.
    ISBN 0-89774-352-0
    1. Economic history—1945– —Bibliography. I. Title.
II. Series.
Z7164.E2H86 1988
[HC59]
016.3309—dc 19   87-35000

Contents

Foreword and Acknowledgements

As a graduate library science student in the late 1950s, and later as a business librarian, I admired Edwin Coman's *Sources of Business Information* so much that I often wondered about doing a similar book. When Professor Paul Wasserman contacted me for this book, I knew this was my opportunity, and one for which I am deeply grateful. For me, it has indeed been a labor of love. Nonetheless, I did not realize that it would be so time consuming and that its preparation would entail such a multitude of obligations. In this brief prefatory note, it is not possible to list all those who have been of assistance, and I ask the indulgence of those not mentioned by name.

I am most obliged to St. John's University for its backing and for allowing me a reduction in teaching load during the academic year 1986–87 to enable me to pursue this work. I owe an abiding indebtedness to Sister Marie Melton, R.S.M., Director of the University Libraries, and to Mrs. Mary Parr, Assistant Director for Technical Services, for their assistance, interest, and encouragement throughout, and, of course, to Dr. Mildred Lowe, former director of the Division of Library and Information Science for her support.

Individuals in many libraries have been of great help. I owe a debt of gratitude to Mr. Amin Abdelsamad, Senior Reference Librarian at the Dag Hammerskjold Library for giving me month-long permission to use the U.N. Library System, and to Ms. Maria Paniagua, also of the U.N. Library Reference Services, for her capable assistance. I wish to express my deep appreciation for all the assistance I received from Ms. Barbara Perry of the World Bank Library, who went out of her way to accommodate me. I am indeed grateful to all the librarians at St. John's University, and particularly to Ms. Arla Lindgren, head of Acquisitions, and Mr. Andrew Sankowski, also of Acquisitions, for ordering some of the books I needed and for their constant encouragement. I am also obliged to my friend and colleague in the Cataloging Department, Mr. Daniel Pierce, for looking over the subject index.

The three people without whom I could not have produced this book are my two graduate assistants and my son. Mrs. Catherine Korvin, assistant for the 1985–86 year, and Ms. Jessica Opatow, for the year 1986–87, have done a superb job in checking, verifying, and locating titles for me. Arefin Huq did all the typing, printing, and occasional editing using a word processor.

I must place on record my appreciation of my wife for making it possible for me to work Saturdays and most evenings for the last year and a half, and also of my nine-year-old daughter, Afrin, for being understanding and letting her brother and dad work all summer while she had to keep herself busy.

Last, but not least, I must thank Carol Hunter, and Jean Bann at The Oryx Press for all of their editorial assistance.

Introduction

During recent times nations of the world have become enmeshed in an interdependent economy, and every state has been exposed to the forces of international economics. Third world nations are now essential participants in the global economic interdependence. The successful functioning of the world economy has come to depend on cooperation, rather than on competition, among nations large or small. Economics dominates everywhere, and it even transcends capitalist and socialist states. This reality has long- as well as short-term implications. Growth and progress in the developing countries has an impact on the developed nations. To contain global economic uncertainties, to sustain economic stability, and to foster economic growth, it is necessary to provide knowledge about the economic conditions of any country or region of the world.

The literature of economics has been growing steadily since the 1970s, and the demand for it has escalated since the 1980s. The global reality requires an outward-looking global perspective with the realization that no nation can chart its economic course alone in a decentralized economic system. A study entitled *Jobs, Growth, and Competitiveness,* prepared by governors Gerard Lee Baliles, Terry E. Branstad, and Michael S. Dukakis (Washington, DC: National Governor's Association, Hall of the States, 1987) and discussed at the 1987 Governor's Conference, made the observation that the key to prosperity is a global view and that Americans are lacking in the understanding of the rest of the world. Thus any attempt to bring together materials relating to world economic conditions should stand in good stead for all those concerned about it. As an instructor for about a decade teaching business and economics literature, I have observed that many American libraries are information-poor in this area. An assignment during the summer of 1986 as a U.N. consultant to set up a library in the field of economics for the Bangladesh government made this author acutely aware of the international economics literature by and about international organizations, their relatively easy availability in countries such as Bangladesh, and the awareness of foreign librarians about such materials. This biliography is an attempt to highlight such literature for librarians everywhere, particularly in the U.S. and other Western nations.

As has been mentioned before, because of the global nature of the economy, it is no longer possible to make any economic decision of significance without appreciation of the happenings elsewhere. While this awakening is taking place, economic decision making has been rendered even more difficult with the oceans of statistics that wash over us every day. It is quite a task to track down such statistics or to be able to locate sources of such statistics and retrieve such data when needed. This requires identifying worldwide economic information sources and organizing them in a way to make access fairly easy. This has been another purpose for compiling this bibliography.

Since the U.N. and its specialized agencies are the main players as well as producers of information in the field of international economics, their publications form a major part of this bibliography. In addition, other specialized agencies, such as the OECD, bring out publications in the field of regional and world economic conditions, and as such their publications also receive due attention.

To identify materials on global economy in printed sources as well as in library catalogs, the term "economic conditions" was used extensively. This may not have been the best choice, but there is no other appropriate term or terms for location of materials on the subject. The *Library of Congress Subject Headings* (LCSH) does not, however, use "economic conditions" as a main heading. It refers to "Economic History" instead, which is not the intended focus of this book. Nevertheless, in the LCSH, "economic conditions" is suggested as a subdivision under goegraphical headings. *The New York Times Index* uses the heading "Economic Conditions and Trends," but about 100 *see also* headings are listed under it. Two major indexing and abstracting services, *Business Periodicals Index* (BPI) and *Public Affairs Information Service Bulletin* (PAIS), use "Economic Conditions," but both also use it as a subheading under geographical areas and other subjects in addition to listing a number of *see also* references. So, it is obvious that this subject is intertwined with a number of other subjects and that materials on this subject in any collection or any printed source are scattered. For optimum results, the Library of Congress classification scheme Class H (subclasses HA, HC and HD, in particular) were consulted frequently.

Selection of sources has been confined to books or book-like publications in the English language, published currently and available in the United States. In the field of economics (as also in business), outdated information, particularly that of a statistical nature, is of little value. Hence, publications prior to 1980 have, in general, been excluded. In exceptional cases, because of the nature of publications, uniqueness, importance, and usefulness, certain items published in the '70s have been included. Selection of periodicals has been restricted to key titles in the subject field. Nonperiodical serials, particularly annuals and yearbooks, have been included whenever they were found appropriate.

All the items in the bibliography were checked against the OCLC Union Catalog, and those found bear the OCLC record number. The presence of an OCLC number, however, does not necessarily mean that the citation matches with the OCLC record in all details nor does it imply that the form of the entry is the same. The form of entry conforms to the publisher's guidelines which include entry under editor(s) for a work produced under editorial direction.

The annotations are both descriptive and evaluative and vary in length. Any time it was felt that some background information would be helpful, or that some perspective would add to the value of the content of the material annotated, such information was provided. Annotations for publications by an organization or a corporate body begin with information about that organization, and such information has been provided under the first entry by that organization. Throughout, the aim has been to try to be helpful to the users in every possible way. No information note has been provided for U.S. government departments or any international agency that are household words everywhere.

Core Library Collection

Encyclopedias

1. *Britannica Book of the Year.* Chicago: Encyclopaedia Britannica, 1938–. (Annual) OCLC 911926.
This updates the *Encyclopaedia Britannica.* In addition to the section "World Data," which is full of statistical information for all countries including the U.S., special reports and feature articles focus on economic conditions. This yearbook is often overlooked for economic and statistical information.

2. Kurian, George Thomas. *Encyclopedia of the Third World.* rev. ed. New York: Facts on File, 1982. 3 vols. OCLC 15090762.
This encyclopedia in three volumes provides a compact, balanced, and objective description of the political, economic, and social systems of the third world. This includes 122 countries and excludes China and Taiwan. According to the author, the third world is no longer a single economic unit but instead is subdivided into at least four easily distinguishable groups: Members of the Organization of Petroleum Exporting Countries; Advanced Developing Countries; Middle Developing Countries; and Less Developing Countries. In the preface, the author provides a short historical overview of the development of the third world and states that the present edition offers not only a broader range of information but also new features that enhance the consultability of the work. All entries are arranged in alphabetical order by the name of the country. The bibliography on the third world is excellent.

3. *Worldmark Encyclopedia of the Nations.* 6th ed. New York: Distributed by John Wiley, 1984. 5 vols. OCLC 10276011.
This is subtitled "A Practical Guide to the Geographic, Historical, Political, Social and Economic Status of All Nations, Their International Relationships, and the United Nations System." It is a multivolume work and revised at intervals ranging from six to eight years. Volume one is devoted to the U.N. itself. Subsequent volumes treat countries and dependencies located in Africa, the Americas, Asia and Oceania, and Europe. A recurring theme in volume one is the U.N.'s overriding interest in development of poorer countries. Coverage of individual nations begins with Algeria in volume two and concludes with Yugoslavia in volume five. The editors

state that the standard treatment of fifty features has been applied uniformly to all countries, regardless of their size, strength, position, or prominence on the world scene. This scheme is a useful means for comparative study and it provides rather balanced knowledge of the new and lesser known nations.

Statistics

4. International Labor Organization (ILO). *Yearbook of Labour Statistics.* Geneva, Switzerland: 1931–. (Annual) OCLC 13198690.
Established in 1919, the ILO became a specialized agency of the United Nations in 1946. Basically, the ILO seeks to improve working and living conditions through the adoption of international labor conventions and recommendations setting standards in such fields as wages, hours of work, conditions of employment, and social security.
  Published annually in December, the yearbook runs to approximately 900 pages and provides labor statistics for over 180 countries and territories for the preceding ten years. Significant changes in format and content have been made in recent editions. The areas of consideration are the total and economically active population, emloyment, unemployment, hours of work, wages, labor costs, consumer prices, occupational injuries, and industrial disputes. Each chapter concentrates on a different facet of labor-related data and is prefaced with an explanation of the scope and methodology of the statistical tables which follow. The arrangement within a subject area is first by continent and then by country.
  This publication has established itself as the world's foremost work of statistical reference on labor-related questions. To facilitate widespread use, three languages are incorporated into the book: English, French, and Spanish. This is updated by two publications: the monthly *International Labor Review* and the quarterly *Bulletin of Labor Statistics.* The former is an excellent source for background information on labor forces throughout the world; the latter, for statistics on employment and unemployment.

5. Kurian, George Thomas. *The New Book of World Rankings.* New York: Facts on File, 1984. 490 p. OCLC 8410872.
As stated in the preface, the output and refinement of international statistics have reached a level where it is possible to convert raw data into indicators of comparative data, which is what the book does for 190 nations in 300 key areas. It is like the *Fortune 500* for nations. The book is divided into twenty-two chapters, including vital statistics, population dynamics and the family, foreign aid, economy, trade, energy, labor, transportation, consumption, housing, health, and food. Much of the available data is stated to have been derived from the publications of the United Nations, the World Bank, the International Monetary Fund, and the U.S. Agency for International Development, all of which do a superb job of collecting international economic statistics.

6. Liesner, Thelma, comp. *Economic Statistics 1900–1983: United Kingdom, United States of America, France, Germany, Italy, Japan.* New York: Facts on File, 1985. 142 p. OCLC 12049825.
This brings together, from a wide variety of sources, basic economic statistics for the leading industrial countries from 1900 and makes them as

consistent as possible. The book is divided into four parts. Part one is the introduction. Part two deals with the U.S. and the U.K. covering 130 statistical series for each country. Part three covers over fifty of the more important statistical series for France, Germany, Italy, and Japan. Part four consists of analytical tables and charts which bring together statistical information from parts two and three so that a comparison is possible. Thus, the book gives a good overview of the economic conditions in the countries mentioned for the present century, although the main emphasis is on the U.K. and the U.S.

7. United Nations Children's Fund (UNICEF). *World Statistics on Children: UNICEF Statistical Pocketbook.* 2d ed. New York, 1986. 91 p.

When it was first established as a temporary body in 1946, UNICEF was known as the U.N. International Children's Emergency Fund. It was placed on a permanent footing in 1953, and the name was changed as above. UNICEF aids programs for child health and maternal and child nutrition.

This pocketbook is the second of a series of annual pocket-size compilations of basic economic and social statistics (i.e., nutrition, health, education, demography, and economics). The white pages of the pocketbook show selected data for some 161 countries for three reference periods: 1960, 1980, and 1983. The colored pages contain world and regional charts and other summary tables on selected topics of primary relevance to the issue of child survival and development.

8. United Nations. Department of International Economic and Social Affairs. *Demographic Yearbook.* New York, 1948–. (Annual) OCLC 1168223.

The yearbook is a compendium of international demographic statistics for over 220 countries and areas. It is designed to supply basic statistical data for demographers, economists, sociologists, and public health workers. Under a cyclical rotation plan of publication, a different field of demographic statistics receives intensive treatment each year. It contains basic data on area, density, population, population growth rates, natality, mortality, expectation of life, nuptiality, marriage, divorce, and international migration. The *Demographic Yearbook, 1985* which features the results of population censuses as the special subject is the thirty-seventh in this series. The special focus of this edition is on international migration. The yearbook is usually published eighteen months after the end of the year to which the data refer. The *Historical Supplement* published in 1980 contains basic population and vital statistics for a thirty-year period.

9. United Nations. Department of International Economic and Social Affairs. *Statistical Indicators on Youth.* New York, 1985. 202 p. OCLC 13642414.

This pocketbook of statistical indicators contains forty such indicators in the following fields: population composition and change; education, training, and literacy; economic activity; family formation and fertility; and life expectancy and mortality. These series cover the years 1970, 1980, and 1985 for 171 countries.

10. United Nations. Department of International Economic and Social Affairs. *Statistical Yearbook.* New York, 1948–. (Annual) OCLC 15096537.

This is possibly the most complete statistical reference book in existence. It is a compilation of international statistics relating to a wide range of economic and social subjects including population; manpower; agricultural and mineral production; construction; energy; trade; transport; consumption; balance of payments; wages and prices; national accounts; public finance; development assistance; health; and housing. It is a compendium of the most important internationally comparative data for the analysis of economic development at the world, regional, and national level. In most cases, at the very least, a run of at least five years of data is given. It represents a convenient source for international statistics in most areas relevant to economics, although the yearbook is slow in being published. Some current figures can be found in the *U.N. Monthly Bulletin of Statistics.* A *Supplement to the Statistical Yearbook* is published from time to time. The 1983–84 edition, published in 1986, is the thirty-fourth issue containing 1,137 pages and 1,134 statistical tables which in many cases cover a ten-year period. The title and the text are in English and French.

11. United Nations. Department of International Economic and Social Affairs. *World Statistics in Brief: United Nations Statistical Pocketbook.* New York, 1976–. (Annual) OCLC 10874110.

Issued annually since 1976, this pocket-size reference book, also known as *Statistical Pocketbook,* is a compilation of basic international statistics. It was undertaken in response to a General Assembly resolution to supply adequate basic national data that would increase the international public's awareness of countries' development efforts. Part of the book shows important and frequently consulted statistical indicators for each of the U.N. member states. Another part contains demographic and economic statistics for the world as a whole, selected regions of the world, and major countries. The 1986 issue covers the years 1975, 1980, and 1984 and in some cases 1983.

12. United Nations. World Health Organization (WHO). *World Health Statistics Annual: 1986.* Geneva, Switzerland, 1986. (Annual) OCLC 15242938.

WHO is one of the original U.N. specialized agencies with headquarters in Geneva. Its task is to help control disease, to promote the highest health standards, to set drug and vaccine standards and health and research guidelines.

In about 700 pages of maps, diagrams, tables, and interpretative text, this book presents a wealth of statistical information useful in monitoring health trends throughout the world. Information ranges from the demographic data on more than 200 countries to statistics on age and sex, to specific death rates by country and by cause. It also features detailed statistical data on a topic of prime relevance to the goal of health for all by the year 2000.

13. United States. Central Intelligence Agency. *The World Factbook.* Washington, DC, 1981–. OCLC 7390695.

Formerly called the *National Basic Intelligence Factbook*, this CIA publication presents a brief review of each country of the world with its most vital information. Coverage for each is anywhere between one and three pages in length and includes information on the country's economy, geography, people, government, and defense. The data are provided by various components of the CIA, the Defense Intelligence Agency, the Bureau of the Census, and the U.S. Department of State. It is a mere collection of data but an excellent ready reference source.

AFRICA

14. Legum, Colin, ed. *Africa Contemporary Record; Annual Survey and Documents.* New York; London: Africa Publishing Co., 1968/69–. (Annual) OCLC 1461370.

This survey examines the social, political, and economic affairs of Africa. The book is divided into three parts. Part one is "Current Issues: Essays," and it chronicles current events with considerable emphasis on economic situations. Part two is a "Country-by-Country Review" of political, social, and economic conditions for each nation. Statistical information is presented in narrative form, but charts and tables are also included. Part three consists of important documents in the political, social, and economic development of the continent. It also covers a wide range of activities including international organizations such as the Organization of African Unity, the United Nations, and the Inter-African Socialist Organization. The book has a subject and a name index.

ASIA

15. *Asia Yearbook.* Hong Kong: Far Eastern Econmic Review, 1973–. (Annual) OCLC 1791821.

Formerly *Far Eastern Economic Review Yearbook*, this is an annual economic, political, and social survey of about thirty countries from China to Sri Lanka. The first third of the book contains regional reviews of politics, food and population, finance and investment, economics, commodities, energy, aviation and shipping, trade, aid, foreign affairs, and refugees. It also discusses World Bank, Asian Development Bank, and other Asian organizations. This is followed by separate sections for each country, each of which contains reviews under the following headings: politics, foreign relations, social affairs, economy, and infrastructure. Beginning with the 1985 yearbook, it introduces a Data Box in each country chapter which includes summary statistical information covering major industrial and agricultural production, imports and exports, finance, and currency conversion figures

16. *Economic Bulletin for Asia and the Pacific.* Bangkok, Thailand: ESCAP Secretariat, 1950–. (Frequency varies, twice yearly since 1976) OCLC 2169163.

Title varies. For the years 1950 to 1970, this used to be called *Economic Bulletin for Asia and the Far East.* It is the journal of the United Nations Economic and Social Commission for Asia and the Pacific (ESCAP). Each issue has a broad, unifying theme. Articles are generally signed and deal with various aspects of the economic development of the region.

17. *The Far East and Australasia.* London: Europa, 1969–. (Annual) OCLC 1345792.

This is an annual reference book on the countries of Asia, including the Soviet Union in Asia, Australia and New Zealand, and the Pacific Islands. In the 1981–82 volume, part one of the book deals with topics including economic growth and development for the entire area. Part two is a survey of the major international organizations concerned with the area. Part three contains information on individual countries. The country profiles include economic and statistical survey.

18. United Nations. Economic and Social Commission for Asia and the Pacific (ESCAP). *Statistical Yearbook for Asia and the Pacific.* Bangkok, Thailand: The Commission, 1970–. (Annual) OCLC 1988344.

Set up by the U.N. in 1947 as the Economic Commission for Asia and the Far East (ECAFE) and changed to the present name in 1974, its headquarters are in Bangkok, with activities including general development, research and advice, and the establishment of regional centers for training and research. Members of the ESCAP consist of states that are within the geographical scope of the commission, which extends from Iran to the Cook Islands together with five nonregional members—France, The Netherlands, the U.S.S.R., the U.K., and the U.S. Non–self–governing territories in the region may become associate members.

Prior to 1974, this yearbook was called the *Statistical Yearbook for Asia and the Far East.* The 1984 volume, the latest available (published in 1986), is the seventeenth issue and contains 630 pages. It is a survey giving detailed economical statistics for thirty-eight countries. It covers population, agriculture, manpower, fisheries, forestry, industry, energy supplies, transportation and communications, expenditure in the public sector, wages, and banking. It is in English and French and is updated by the *Quarterly Bulletin of Statistics for Asia and the Pacific.*

China

19. People's Republic of China. State Statistical Bureau, comp. *Statistical Yearbook of China, 1981.* Hong Kong: Economic Information and Agency, 1982. 524 p. OCLC 9403365.

It contains statistical data of China's economic and social development in 1981 as well as the major statistical indicators of the preceding thirty-one years or in some cases since the founding of the People's Republic. Statistics relating to Taiwan are in the appendix and not shown as part of the nationwide statistics, unless otherwise indicated in the text. A revised, enlarged, and updated 1986 edition is scheduled for publication shortly.

Japan

20. *Japan Economic Almanac, 1986.* Tokyo, Japan: Japan Economic Journal, 1986. 294 p.
It covers all facets of Japan's economy and trade. It is full of statistical tables, charts, and graphics. In the "Data and Statistics" section, in addition to providing essential economic statistics, a directory of the Japanese government appears.

CANADA

21. Canada. Statistics Canada. *Canadian Statistical Review.* Ottawa, ON, 1926–. (Monthly) OCLC 2480633.
This is considered to be the best source for Canadian socioeconomic information. This began as a bilingual (English and French) in 1926. Separate English and French editions have been published since 1948. The Bureau of Statistics issued it through July 1971, and Statistics Canada has published it since August 1971. One of its many useful features is an analytical summary of selected economic indicators, namely, Gross National Product, Personal Expenditure on Consumer Goods and Services, Current Account Balance, and much more. It has published occasional annual supplements.

22. *The Corpus Almanac of Canada.* Toronto, ON: Corpus Publishers Services, 1966–. (Annual) OCLC 1476046.
Compared to the other almanac, *Canadian Almanac and Directory*, this is considered to be superior. However, one troublesome feature of this almanac is that it has significant changes from edition to edition based on the supposed needs of the users. Its policy is to add new topics each year and drop others that become available from other sources. In any case, it generally has a section on finance, taxation, labor, and transportation.

EUROPE

23. *The Europa Yearbook 1985: A World Survey.* London: Europa Publications, 1985, 2 vols. (Annual)
This yearbook was first published in 1926. Beginning in 1960, it has been a two-volume publication. It is widely known as a general international reference tool. It is also full of useful economic information. Volume one deals with international organizations and countries of Europe as well as provides the first part of the alphabetical survey of the rest of the world. Volume two lists the remaining countries of the world. The data provided for each country usually includes economic affairs, basic economic statistics, recent history, constitution, government, political parties, etc. Tables provide current statistics and list references to original sources.

Eastern Europe

24. *East European Economic Handbook.* London: Euromonitor, 1985. 325 p. OCLC 12973926.
This is the first Euromonitor's series of economic studies. It gives an overview of the region, its role in the world economy, and its prospects for the future. The book is divided into ten chapters. Chapter one covers the region in the world context along with a review of its economic performance compared with other areas of the world. Chapter two gives the regional overview with comparative economic performance in 1980. The remaining chpaters contain profiles of individual countries. These are followed by a statistical appendix of twenty tables.

European Communities

25. European Communities (EC). Eurostat. *Basic Statistics of the Community: Comparison with Some European Countries, Canada, the U.S.A., Japan, and the U.S.S.R.* 24th ed. Luxembourg, 1987. 293 p. OCLC 10821126.
European Community was formed by merging the three European communities: European Coal and Steel Community (ECSC), European Atomic Energy Community (Euratom), and the European Economic Community (EEC). In 1973, the six founder members (Belgium, France, Italy, Luxembourg, The Netherlands, and Germany) were joined by Denmark, Ireland, and the U.K. Greece became a member in 1981, and Portugal and Spain in 1986. The European Community aims to break down trade barriers within a common market and to create a political union among the peoples of Europe.
    The above volume is a handy statistical publication compiled by the Statistical Office of the European Community (Eurostat). In this pocketbook edition, more than half the pages are devoted to economics and related matters. For a worldwide comparison of industrialized countries, it is perhaps unsurpassed as a publication of this magnitude.

Great Britain

26. *The Economist.* London, 1843–. (Weekly) OCLC 1081684.
This longtime venerable weekly of British origin contains feature articles and news on economic and political trends, focusing primarily on the U.K. but also covering Europe, the international scene, and the U.S. A great deal of information is packed into relatively short and highly readable articles.

27. Great Britain. Central Office of Information. *Britain, 1987: An Official Handbook.* London: Her Majesty's Stationary Office, 1987. 468 p. (Annual) OCLC 15564039.
This is the thirty-eighth edition in this series. It describes many features of the life of the country including its economy. In addition to a chapter on "National Economy," there are other chapters that contain information of interest to students of the subject, e.g., Social Welfare, Environment,

Framework of Industry, Agriculture, Fisheries and Forestry, and Employment. The handbook is updated every year to include latest facts and figures from official sources.

28. *The Statesman's Year-Book; Statistical and Historical Annual of the States of the World.* London: Macmillan, 1864–. (Annual)
It has long been a standard reference work throughout the world, particularly for information on the United Kingdom and the Commonwealth. It appears in a new edition each year and attempts to cover the major facts about every country of the world. It surveys a variety of topics, including economics, and supplies comparative statistical data. This work crams a wealth of information into a small volume and is relatively more up to date than similar publications.

29. Whitaker, Joseph. *An Almanack for the Year of Our Lord 1984.* London: Whitaker, 1984. 1,220 p. (Annual)
This is subtitled "Containing an Account of the Astronomical and Other Phenomena and a Vast Amount of Information Respecting the Government, Finance, Population, Commerce, and General Statistics of the Various Nations of the World, with an Index Containing Nearly 22,000 References." This is the one hundred sixteenth edition. It is a general information almanac concentrating on the United Kingdom and the Commonwealth. It has considerable economic information and statistics, but these are difficult to locate despite a sixty-three-page subject index.

U.S.S.R.

30. U.S.S.R. Central Statistical Board. *The USSR in Figures for 1985: Brief Statistical Handbook.* Moscow, U.S.S.R.: Finansy Statistika Publishers, 1986. 253 p. (Annual) OCLC 10227578.
This is an annual and contains statistical returns on the economic and social developments of the U.S.S.R. for 1985 with comparative figures for 1940, 1960, 1970, 1975, 1980, and, for the most part, for other years as well. It is also available in French, German, and Spanish.

MIDDLE EAST

31. *The Middle East and North Africa.* London: Europa Publications, 1948–. (Annual, but irregular during 1948 through 1959) OCLC 2473588.
Title varies. It began as *The Middle East* and changed to its present title with the 1964–65 edition. This is a major reference source covering the Middle East and North Africa. Part one is a general survey including the economy of the region. Part two covers regional organizations involved in the area including the Economic Commission for Africa, Economic Commission for Western Asia, other U.N. agencies, and international agencies such as the OPEC Fund for International Development, and Arab Bank for Economic Development in Africa. Part three provides country profiles giving economical, geographical, historical, and statistical information. Part

four contains reference materials such as a Who's Who listing, research institutes, and bibliography.

32. Sinclair, Stuart W. *Middle East Economic Handbook.* London: Euromonitor Publications, 1986. 487 p.

The book begins with an overview of the Middle East in the world context, then proceeds to give an overview of the economic and political forces at work in the major Middle East countries. This is followed by country profiles of each of the countries in the region, and finally, a future outlook of the Middle Eastern economies is given. The statistical appendix provides a basic set of data for the years 1980 through 1984 that enables comparison among these countries.

SOUTH AMERICA

33. Blakemore, Harold. *South American Economic Handbook.* London: Euromonitor, 1986. 274 p. OCLC 13669558.

It contains an overview of the economic conditions in South America. Chapter one discusses the region in the world context and highlights a comparative economic performance with other regions of the world. Chapter two gives a regional overview followed by profiles of the thirteen countries that make up South America. The profile of each country includes a discussion of the structure of the economy, its agriculture, industry, foreign investments, and trade. Pertinent statistical tables are supplied. In the final chpater, there is a general discussion of the economic outlook for the region with a summary for the six major economies: Argentina, Brazil, Chile, Colombia, Peru, and Venezuela. There is a statistical appendix for a comparative review of the economic conditions and performance of all the South American countries.

34. United Nations. Economic Commission for Latin America (ECLAC). *Statistical Yearbook for Latin America and the Caribbean.* 1985 ed. Santiago, Chile: ECLAC, 1986. OCLC 14147215.

This yearbook, with its various titles, was set up by the U.N. in 1948, with headquarters in Santiago, to carry out research and provide advice on economic development in Latin America. It works closely with the many regional intergovernmental organizations including the Organization of American States (OAS), the Latin American Economic System (LAES), and the Latin American Integration Association (LAIA). Membership in the commission is open to members of the U.N. in North, Central, and South America and in the Caribbean, and to France, The Netherlands, Portugal, Spain, and the U.K.

For the years 1975 through 1984, this publication was titled *Statistical Yearbook for Latin America* with a parallel Spanish title. The 1985 edition reflects a major effort to speed the delivery of statistical information concerning the region. The ECLAC maintains a computerized database, and that portion of the database used in the yearbook is maintained online. Despite computerization, the format of tables and its arrangement of topics and subtopics are the same as in earlier editions. Although thirty-two countries are members of ECLAC, data are generally listed for twenty-four, and for the remaining eight, data are rather scarce.

UNITED STATES

Almanacs

35. *The Business Week Almanac.* New York: McGraw-Hill, 1982–. OCLC 8496981.
This is the first edition of the almanac. It is an instant reference source for such diverse subjects as banking, energy, environment, government, interest rates, investments and securities, labor, law, real estate, stocks and bonds, taxes and personal income, to mention a few of the many topics covered in this information package.

36. *The Dow Jones-Irwin Business and Investment Almanac.* Homewood, IL: Dow Jones-Irwin, 1971–. (Annual) OCLC 8188096.
This is a compact and comprehensive reference book on business, finanace, and economics providing not only up-to-date statistics but also detailed anlayses of them. New features are added in each edition to keep up with current developments and topics of interest. Among the new features in the 1986 edition are government budgets, receipts, and deficits. It includes general business and economic indicators, industry surveys and financial data.

37. *Information Please Almanac.* New York: Doubleday, 1947–. (Annual) OCLC 14909814.
This is an almanac of general information but includes extensive statistical and economic information on the United States. In addition, it provides statistical and historical descriptions of the various countries of the world and many kinds of general information. Subjects are alphabetically arranged in the main section, and sources for many of the tables and special articles are noted. This almanac is often compared with the *World Almanac and Book of Facts,* and both have much the same information although packaged differently. Whether one is better than the other depends on the orientation and the type of information needed.

38. *The World Almanac and Book of Facts.* New York: Newspaper Enterprise Association, 1868–. (Annual) OCLC 912524.
Some consider this almanac to be the most comprehensive and most useful of the American general information almanacs. It has a history going back under various publishers and is now published by the Newspaper Enterprise Association. With a general reference index in the back of the book and a detailed index in the front, it is rather easy to consult. It begins with a news summary of the previous year and contains statistics on social, industrial, economical, financial, and other subjects. Sources of many of the statistics are given.

Handbooks and Guides

39. *The Handbook of Basic Economic Statistics: A Manual of Basic Economic Data on Industry, Commerce, Labor, and Agriculture in the United States.* Washington, DC: Economic Statistics Bureau of Washington, DC, 1947–. (Annual, with monthly supplements)

This is a paperback compilation of basic economic statistics on the U.S. economy, industry, commerce, labor, and agriculture, condensed from the federal government data covering more than 1,800 statistical series. Data go back 1913 or the first year thereafter for which figures are available. It is stated that most statistics are presented two to four weeks in advance of formal government publication.

40. Rand McNally & Company. *Rand McNally Commercial Atlas & Marketing Guide, 1987.* 118th ed. Chicago, 1987. (Annual) OCLC 15141399.

According to the statement on the front cover, it is the best, first place to look for economic data, transportation and communication data, population estimates and summaries, statistics, and indexes for every populated area in the U.S. The maps are clear and large.

41. United States. Bureau of Industrial Economics. *U.S. Industrial Outlook, 1987.* Washington, DC: U.S. Government Printing Office, 1987. (Annual) OCLC 10482680.

Issued annually since 1960, it presents an overview of the current status for most manufacturing and service industries in the United States, based on data from the previous year, outlook for the current year, and projections for the next five years. Each chapter begins with an analysis of the industry group based on its performance over the past several years, discusses the current situation, and gives short- and long-term prospects. The industries included in each group are then treated individually. Trends accompany the narrative description for most industries. Many of the annual editions contain an analysis of several dozen rapid-growth industries, and their prospects are given. Selected industries are also ranked by their annual percent of change in shipments.

42. United States. Bureau of Labor Statistics. *Handbook of Labor Statistics.* Washington, DC: U.S. Government Printing Office, 1924–. (Annual) OCLC 10580163.

This handbook makes available in one volume the major statistical series produced by the bureau and contains extensive data on employment. The nearly 200 tables are grouped under the following topics: labor force, employment and unemployment, special labor force data, employees on nonagricultural payrolls, other employment surveys, productive data, compensation studies, prices and living conditions, unions and industrial relations, occupational injuries and illnesses, foreign labor statistics, and general economic data. Each table is historically complete, beginning with the earliest reliable and consistent data, and running through the current calendar year. Related series from other governmental agencies and foreign countries are included. Because the data are grouped under headings having economic significance, comparison of the series becomes easy.

43. United States. Bureau of the Census. *Statistical Abstract of the United States.* Washington, DC: U.S. Government Printing Office, 1878–. (Annual) OCLC 1193890.

This is perhaps the best place to begin a search for economic statistical data for the United States. It is an economic treasure trove presenting facts and figures on virtually all aspects of the American social and economic life. Published annually since 1878, it collects important summary statistics from federal and nongovernmental agencies in a volume which generally exceeds 1,000 pages. Tables are annotated as to source, indicating what agency or agencies were responsible for the data. It also contains an excellent statistical bibliography in the appendix. It has a comprehensive subject index. Although the figures in this abstract usually cover just one or a few years, the bureau also publishes a useful historical supplement called *Historical Statistics of the United States: Colonial Times to 1970.*

Periodicals

44. *Business Week.* New York: McGraw-Hill, September 7, 1929–. (Weekly) OCLC 1537921.

It is one of the most well-known business and economic magazines published in the United States. In concisely written articles, this weekly covers all facets of domestic and international economics and business. The articles are grouped into sections such as "Economic Analysis," "Finance," "Industry and Technology," and "International" Usually, one long article is featured in each issue, plus there are regular columns such as "Figures of the Week." Annually or quarterly, about seven different lists of leading companies provide useful financial statistics mostly arranged by industry. The layout of this magazine is interesting, and the color is used effectively, especially in the tables and charts.

45. *Fortune.* New York: Time Inc., February 1930–. (Biweekly) OCLC 1569892.

Like *Business Week, Fortune* is another well-known business and economics magazine published in the United States. A typical issue might include one or two articles on a U.S. or foreign company; one on an economic or financial problem, or the past, present, and anticipated condition of the American economy; or one on a new technology or strategy. Each issue also contains economic forecasts and a column on personal investing. This journal is widely known for its several lists of rankings each year, the most notable being the *Fortune 500.*

46. United States Board of Governors of the Federal Reserve System. *Federal Reserve Bulletin.* Washington, DC, 1915–. (Monthly) OCLC 1606526.

This is considered to be the official voice of the Federal Reserve System. It is the best single source for finding current U.S. banking and monetary statistics including federal finance, interest rates on money and capital markets, stock market indexes, mortgages, flow of funds, consumer installment credit, interest and exchange rates, international financial statistics, and basic U.S. business statistics including the well-known Federal Reserve Board's index of industrial production. About half of each issue is devoted to the presentation of financial and business statistics. The other half usually includes articles, one or more reports to the Congress, and position papers that make known the views and policies of the Federal Reserve system. Each issue also contains reports on the transactions of the Federal Open Market Committee responsible for setting the nation's monetary policy. Most statistics in the bulletin are based on reports made to the board or from the U.S. Treasury Department. Each issue also has a short section for "International Statistics" which includes, among other topics, summary data on international transactions, U.S. reserve assets, liabilties to and claims on unaffiliated foreigners reported by U.S. banks and by nonbank enterprises, foreign interest, and exchange rates.

47. United States. Bureau of Economic Analysis. *Survey of Current Business.* Washington, DC: U.S. Government Printing Office, 1921–. (Monthly) OCLC 1697070.

It is the most important and possibly the most used government publication in the field of economics. It provides data and analysis on the current condition of the U.S. economy and business. It contains the most extensive breakdown of current National Income and Product Accounts (NIPA) values. In addition, it provides current information for every series in the biennial *Business Statistics* and brings *Statistical Abstract of the United States* up to date.

48. United States. Council of Economic Advisors. *Economic Indicators.* Washington, DC, May 1948–. (Monthly) OCLC 1567401.

The contents are made up entirely of economic data prepared in the form of tables and charts. The monthly issuance of this title allows it to present the state of the economic health of the United States on as current a basis as possible. It is the best single current source on a variety of leading and lagging economic indicators for the United States. This updates the annual report *Economic Report of the President.*

WORLD ECONOMY

49. Carlip, Vivian; Overstreet, William; and Linder, Dwight, ed. *Economic Handboook of the World 1982.* New York: Published for the Center for Social Analysis of the State University of New York at Binghampton by McGraw-Hill, 1982. (Annual) OCLC 7157109.

Changes in editorship from 1981 edition. This presents a comprehensive overview and a current analysis of the economies of all countries in the world, from Afganistan to Zimbabwe. It opens with an introductory essay on "The World Economy," and continues to "The National Economies," under which all the countries are covered. Each country profile begins with summary statistics followed by a narrative, usually with the following sections: the setting, structure of the economy, domestic trends, trade and foreign investment, future direction, and principal economic institutions. Summary statistics for each country generally include area, population, GNP, international reserves, external debt, government revenue, expenditure, and consumer prices. The last part of the book deals with international organizations, followed by two appendices.

50. Economist Intelligence Unit (Great Britain). *The World in Figures.* New York: Facts on File, 1980. 294 p. OCLC 5726520.

This is a comprehensive statistical guide to the world and its nations containing essential economic information, compiled by the prestigious British Journal at *The Economist,* from a wide variety of sources. It presents fascinating comparisons among nations (a forty-five-page section of world statistics) as well as in-depth profiles of over 200 countries. The volume is divided into two main sections: a world section and a section of individual countries. Countries are grouped in the second section by main region, and a country name index is included at the back of the book for easy reference; this index also includes alternative names and old names for various countries. In this book, estimates are marked with an asterisk or asterisks, and a gradation has been introduced to give some indication of the possible degree of error, e.g., one asterisk means provisional or estimate, and two asterisks mean rough estimate.

51. International Monetary Fund (IMF). *World Economic Outlook: A Survey by the Staff of the International Monetary Fund.* Washington DC, 1980–. (Annual) OCLC 7621785.

The IMF was founded as one of the Bretton Woods Institutions in 1944. It is the nearest equivalent to a world central bank. It began operation in 1947. The fund's real task is to help smooth monetary relationships between member countries; promote monetary cooperation, currency stabilization, and trade expansion; and meet balance of payments difficulties.

This is a survey conducted by the IMF staff which summarizes recent and prospective developments in the world economy. The report is a unique blend of individual country insights as well as global perspectives. It consists of several chapters supported by supplementary notes as background documentation and a statistical appendix. The report discusses the problems of balance of payments adjustments by the major groups of countries, the key policy options available to them, issues of inflation and interest rates, debt, and capital flows. In addition, the report features detailed scenarios for the evolution of the world economy. The projection and analyses contained in the outlook are the product of a comprehensive interdepartmental review of economic developments by the staff of IMF. This review is carried out annually and draws on the information the fund staff gathers through its regular and special consultations with member countries. It has been published annually since 1980, and beginning 1984 a shorter, updated version of it containing revised projections has also been published in the second half of the year.

52. Sinclair, Stuart W. *Third World Economic Handbook.* London: Euromonitor Publications 1982. 198 p. OCLC 9115560.

This book presents an overview of the economic state of the third world at the start of the 1980s. Aware of the fact that the third world is not a homogenous entity, it deals separately with various groupings that have certain common characteristics. The book begins with an introductory chapter that discusses the state of the third world in 1982. Chapter two then examines the prospects for one particular subgroup, the member of the OPEC whose gradual success since 1960, and more spectacularly since 1973, has made them some of the most significant third world locations of business opportunities. Chapter three follows by examining a second set of countries which have increasingly become distinguished from the bulk of the third world by virtue of their rapid growth of economic and industrial capacity. Chapter four next analyzes a selection of the remaining middle income countries. Chapter five briefly reviews the position in the thirty-one so-called least developed countries. Chapter six draws together the most important conclusions from the body of the book. In sum, the book considers the current position of the developing economies and how they reacted to the two oil crises of the 1970s, the speed and extent of their industrialization, financial trends, and their involvement in world trade; and compares their economic growth with that of the developed economies. Statistics presented for each country include all the major economic and demographic variables relating to development. The separate statistical appendix provides a key source of comparative data.

53. United Nations. Department of International Economic and Social Affairs. *World Economic Survey, 1987: Current Trends and Policies in World Economy.* New York, 1987. 182 p. (Annual) OCLC 9242680.
Title and subtitle vary. This is the fortieth issue in a continuing annual series, the first of which was published in 1947. At that time, it was among the first attempts to provide a comprehensive view of the global economic situation. The task of each survey has been to analyze the major current issues in the world economy that require attention and action by the international community. In the present survey, the topics raised are macroeconomic policy coordination, international trade, international finance and debt, world energy markets, redirection of policies in planned economies, sources of economic growth in developing countries, and persistent unemployment in some developed market economies. Forecasts are made for key global variables for 1987 and 1988. The 1987 survey and other recent issues take a forward-looking, more analytical, and less descriptive approach than earlier ones. It ought to be pointed out that the U.N. is organized into separate "Economic and Social Commissions" for various geographic regions—Africa, Asia and the Pacific, Europe, and Latin America—and each publishes various periodic economic surveys and/or economic bulletins reviewing and analyzing developments in countries of the region.

54. World Bank. *World Bank Atlas.* Washington, DC, 1966–. (Annual) OCLC 13831709.
The World Bank Group comprises the bank itself, officially named the International Bank for Reconstruction and Development and its two affiliates, the International Development Association and the International Finance Corporation. The bank was founded at the Bretton Woods Monetary and Financial Conference in 1944 and began operation in 1946. It is a specialized agency of the United Nations, as are its two affiliates. At present, the bank is the largest multilateral source of development financing in the world. The bank, owned by over 140 member governments, is based in Washington, DC.
   The subtitle of the above publication varies. In keeping with the previous editions, the 1987 issue presents current economic and social indicators that describe trends and indicate orders of magnitude and charcterizes significant differences between countries. It presents data on population, GNP, and GNP per capita for 1985 in current U.S. dollars. It also presents estimates for each of these indicators for 1985 and annual growth rates for 1973–85. It covers 184 countries and provides global and

regional maps along with a breakdown of statistics. Texts, charts, and color-keyed maps highlight some of the more instructive aspects of the data for each of the six economic and social indicators.

55. World Bank. *World Development Report.* New York: Oxford University Press, 1978–. (Annual) OCLC 4227367.
This report is an annual reference to the world economy. *The Guardian* has called it "the nearest thing to having an annual report on the present state of the planet and the people who live on it." Each issue contains an overview of the state of development and a detailed analysis of a related topic. One admirable feature of this publication is its statistical annex called "World Development Indicators" which provides information about the main features of economic and social development trends in countries. Rates of growth and ratios are given to illustrate trends. To facilitate comparison, the median value of the indicators is shown for each country group. The following types of information are generally included in the tables: population; per capita and its growth; changes in food and energy production and consumption per capita; inflation rates; growth and structure of production and demand; growth structure and direction of trade; the balance of payments, capital flows, debt, and aid; developments in the labor force; and health conditions, availability of health, and education services.
The 1987 edition of this annual publication, in addition to the standard features of this series, examines the effects of foreign trade on the pace and scale of industrialization. The final portion of the book, "World Development Indicators," contains thirty-three statistical tables giving economic and social profiles of 128 countries. It is indeed an excellent source for readily accessibly data on world economy. Also available in Arabic, Chinese, French, German, Japanese, Portuguese, and Spanish

56. World Bank. *World Tables.* 3d ed. Baltimore, MD: Johns Hopkins University Press, 1984. 2 vols. OCLC 10275609.
From the data files of the World Bank, it presents economic statistics for developing countries and industrialized market economies that are World Bank members. The 1983 edition, like its predecessors in 1976 and 1980, presents time series for individual countries in absolute numbers for the basic economic variables—population, national accounts, prices, balance of payments, external public debt, foreign trade indexes, and central government finance—as well as economic and social indicators in a form suitable for cross-country analysis and comparison. Although the World Bank is largely concerned with its developing member countries comparable statistical information for countries with developed market economies are also included in the tables to provide a global perspective. The publication includes extensive technical notes; glossary; translation of headings into French and Spanish; and classification of developing countries by income group and geographic region, of industrialized countries, and of centrally planned economies.

57. World Resources Institute, and the International Institute for Environment and Development. *World Resources, 1986.* New York: Basic Books, 1986. 353 p. OCLC 13124707.
This volume, the first in an annual series, is a joint undertaking of two prestigious research organizations, one based in London, and the other in

Washington, DC. It draws on more than 100 statistical reviews and assessments of global and regional resources published by international agencies such as the U.N., the World Bank, regional organizations such as the Economic Commission for Europe, and national government reports. The volume includes comprehensive data for 146 countries. Separate chapters provide concise accounts of the latest developments in population, food and agriculture, human settlements, forests, wildlife and habitat, energy, freshwater, oceans and coasts, atmosphere and climate, and policies and institutions. This report covers the recent past and the present. This extensive coverage and the wealth of facts make it an indispensable reference tool for anyone interested in the global prospect.

Topical Literature

AGED

58. Burtless, Gary. *Work, Health, and Income among the Elderly.* Washington, DC: Brookings Institution, 1987. OCLC 14719499.
The research reported in this volume addresses a variety of policy issues relating to the work and health status of the aged and to the adequacy of income and food consumption among older households. A central issue raised is whether rapid gains in longevity have led to greater frailty in the elderly population.

59. United Nations. Department of International Economic and Social Affairs. *The World Aging Situation: Strategies and Policies.* New York, 1985. 301 p. OCLC 12736213.
The report is divided into three parts: part one, "Global Overview," focuses on global demographic change, aging issues, and policy options; part two provides regional analyses; and part three lists tasks for the future. It has fifty-six tables of statistics. By bringing together relevant data from the abundance of new national, regional, and internationally oriented literature stimulated by the World Assembly on Aging (Vienna, July 26 to August 6, 1982), the present report provides a comprehensive picture of the world aging situation including current and projected demographic trends and estimates of their socioeconomic and humanitarian implications.

60. Zopf, Paul E. *America's Older Population.* Houston, TX: Cap and Gown Press, 1986. 325 p. OCLC 12236752.
This examines the characteristics of older people and the ways in which those characteristics are interwoven, using data for 1980 and later years. The study is comparative, contrasting America's elderly population with those in other societies. Within the United States, it compares men and women, blacks and whites, Hispanics and non-Hispanics, and rural and urban people. It assesses the social, economic, political, and other results of the processes of aging in America's population, basically along two lines: (1) the impact that the elderly and their characteristics have on society, and (2) the consequences that those characteristics have for the elderly themselves. The book emphasizes social demography, which brings together the data and methods of the demographer and the insights and concerns of the humanist. The topics in the book are as follows: (1) Number and Distribution of Older People; (2) Age Composition; (3) Sex Composition; (4) Marriage and Family Status; (5) Educational Status; (6)

Work Characteristics; (7) Retirement; (8) Income and Poverty Status; (9) Mortality Levels, Differentials, and Trends; (10) Internal Migration; and (11) Some Implications of America's Aging Population. Most chapters of the book offer projections, meant to be a contribution to rational social planning for the numbers and proportions of older people who will be part of American society well into the next century and for the needs they and the working population will have. The statistical tables are superb in what they present and how they are presented.

AGRICULTURE

61. United Nations Economic Commission for Europe (ECE). *The Forest Resources of the ECE Region (Europe, the USSR, North America).* Geneva, Switzerland, 1985. 223 p. OCLC 13046707.
This is prepared under the auspices of the Joint FAO/ECE Working Party on Forest Economics and Statistics. The commission is composed of the European members of the U.N., plus Switzerland, U.S., and Canada. The publication consists of three parts: part one, "General Forest Resource Inventory Data"; part two, "The Volume and Mass of Tree and Other Woody Biomass"; and part three, "The Role of the Forest in Supplying Environmental and Other Non-Wood Goods and Services." Part one, which includes basic statistics, forest area, growing stock, fellings, and removals, may be of general interest, and part three may be of special interest to environmentalists.

62. United Nations. Food and Agriculture Organization (FAO). *Atlas of the Living Reources of the Seas.* Prepared by the FAO Fisheries Department. Rome, Italy, 1981. 23 p.83 leaves. OCLC 11157744.
The FAO was established in 1945. Its purpose is to increase the efficiency of the production and distribution of all food and agricultural products and to improve the condition of the rural population and to raise levels of nutrition in developing countries and thus contribute toward the expanding world economy.
The atlas shows the distribution of the principal living resources of the sea. First published in 1971, the atlas has been revised and expanded to include recent information on fishery resources and their variations in time and space. It is an essential reference tool for everyone concerned with ocean resources. It is trilingual: English, French, and Spanish.

63. United Nations. Food and Agriculture Organization (FAO). *FAO Fertilizer Yearbook.* Rome, Italy, 1978–. (Annual)
Title varies prior to 1978. The 1985 volume, published in 1986, is the thirty-fifth edition in this series. This is an annual report on world production, trade, consumption, and prices of fertilizers. Each edition includes the most current data available. It is trilingual: English, French, and Spanish.

64. United Nations. Food and Agriculture Organization (FAO). *Forest Products: World Outlook Projections, 1985–2000.* Rome, Italy, 1986. 101 p. OCLC 15042247.
This shows the projection of consumption and production of modern sector forest products. It is based on data of the *FAO Yearbook of Forest Products, 1961–1984.* The tables show the actual data for 1984 and projections to 1990, 1995, and 2000. Text is also in French and Spanish.

65. United Nations. Food and Agriculture Organization (FAO). *1984 Country Tables: Basic Data on the Agricultural Sector.* Rome, Italy, 1984. 382 p.
The purpose of these tables is to provide important data in concise form. These tables include estimates of total population, national accounts including gross domestic product, and socioeconomic indicators. An updated version of these tables is issued at the beginning of each year. It is trilingual: English, French, and Spanish.

66. United Nations. Food and Agriculture Organization (FAO). *Production Yearbook.* Rome, Italy, 1948–. (Annual) OCLC 1569624.
This annual presents data on all important aspects of food and agriculture, including population, index numbers of agricultural production, food supplies, wages, and freight rates. The information is by countries, continents, economic classes, and regions of the world, for a five-year average, and also for the three most recent years. The 1985 volume has 131 statistical tables listed under various headings of land, crops, livestock, numbers and products, food supply, means of production, prices, and statistical summary. This yearbook is trilingual: English, French, and Spanish. The FAO also publishes a *Monthly Bulletin of Statistics* which updates the tables published in the yearbook. The bulletin also contains articles of topical interest on economic aspects.

67. United Nations. Food and Agriculture Organization (FAO). *World Agricultural Statistical: FAO Statistical Pocketbook.* Rome, Italy, 1986. 187 p. OCLC 14939387.
This publication provides the most important indicators relating to agriculture, fishery, forestry, and food. The purpose of this pocketbook is to present this information in a concise and internationally comparable form for each country as well as for continents, economic classes, regions, and the world. Information is shown for the years 1965, 1970, 1975, 1980, and 1984 together with the corresponding exponential growth rates for 1965 through 1984. It is in French, English, and Spanish, but there is a title and a short appendix in Arabic.

68. United Nations. Food and Agriculture Organization (FAO). *World Food Report, 1986.* Rome, Italy, 1986.
Begun in 1983, it provides an up-to-date briefing on the world food and agriculture situation. It also reviews the work of the FAO during the previous year. It includes general background information on current topics of interest in food and agricultural development.

69. United Nations. Food and Agriculture Organization (FAO). *Yearbook of Fishery Statistics*. Rome, Italy, 1947–. (Annual) OCLC 1770315.

Since 1964, it has been published in two volumes. The volume subtitled "Catches and Landings" covers data on quantities of fish caught, broken down by countries, species, and fishing areas, for recent years including the year of publication. The volume subtitled "Fishery Commodities" covers disposition of catches and both production and international trade data by types of fishery commodities. This also covers recent years including the year of publication, and the data are broken down by countries. For the imports and exports, both quantity and value are given. The *Bulletin of Fishery Statistics*, an irregular serial, supplements the yearbook.

70. United Nations. Food and Agriculture Organization (FAO). *Yearbook of Forest Products*. Rome, Italy, 1947–. (Annual)

This began in 1947 as a bilingual publication under the title *Yearbook of Forest Product Statistics* and changed to its present title in 1967, when it became a trilingual (English, French, and Spanish) publication. This annual publication, compiled by the FAO in collaboration with the Economic Commission for Europe (ECE), covers the two latest years of data on production and trade in forest products for about 180 countries. The 1986 issue is arranged in three parts. The first part contains tables dealing with the volume of production and the volume and value of trade. The second part contains tables dealing with the direction of trade based on export data. These trade matrices show all countries with a total export trade amounting to at least 1 percent of the total. All major world exports are identified with an exporting country and importing country. The third part contains tables showing the unit value in trade of some commodities. These have been obtained by dividing total value by total volume traded.

71. United Nations. International Fund for Agricultural Development (IFAD). *Annual Report, 1985*. Rome, Italy, 1986. 151 p.

The establishement of IFAD was among the proposals from the 1974 World Food Conference. IFAD was inducted in 1977 with about $1 billion from industrialized countries and from OPEC to raise food production and consumption by the poorest people in the poorest countries.

This report is a highly informative and statistical document on the international situation, dealing with global approaches to development and international economic order. The primary focus is on debt and growth crises and IFAD aid flows to developing countries. IFAD has been described as the United Nations agency that plants pride, sows self-reliance, and harvests hope around the world.

CHILDREN

72. Grant, James P. *The State of the World's Children 1984*. New York: Published for UNICEF by Oxford University Press, 1983. (Annual) OCLC 11088248.

In recent years, UNICEF's annual *State of the World's Children Report* has been the most welcome publication about world development. The 1983 report set out its most important message: recent breakthroughs have made it possible to save the lives of up to seven million children a year and to prevent an equal number from becoming mentally or physically disabled. The 1984 report describes the worldwide response to the challenge of this "revolution for children." Part three of the book presents basic economic and social statistics concerning children on all countries of the world.

73. United Nations. Department of International Economic and Social Affairs. *Selected Demographic and Social Characteristics of the World's Children and Youth.* New York, 1986. 108 p. OCLC 13746296.
This presents a description of selected demographic and social characteristics of the world's children and youth, their number, growth, composition, mortality levels, cause of death patterns, sex differentials in mortality, contribution to internal migation in both less developed and more developed regions, and levels of illiteracy and educational attainment in developing countries.

74. World Bank. *World Atlas of the Child.* Washington, DC, 1979. 39 p.
This presents a global portrait of the children of 185 countries. It is a collection of maps highlighting child-related data on GNP and population; number of children, aged birth to fourteen years; crude birth rates and number of births; life expectancy at birth; infant mortality; children in the labor force; primary and secondary education enrollment; and pupil/teacher ratios in primary education. The introduction to the book is in English, French, and Spanish. Although out of date, it is still valuable for its graphic presentation.

CITIES AND TOWNS

75. Gappert, Gary, ed. *The Future of Winter Cities.* Beverly Hills, CA: Sage Publications, 1986. 337 p. OCLC 13185558.
This is volume thirty-one in the Urban Affairs Annual Reviews series. This is a series of reference volumes discussing programs, policies, and current developments in all areas of concern to urban specialists. This volume assesses the prospects for snow belt cities in the United States, Canada, and elsewhere in the world. The book is divided into three parts. Part one is an analysis of the cold cities. The analysis identifies the particular role of annexation in the growth of southern cities and indicates that the loss of employment in northern cities may have peaked in the last decade. In this regard another volume in this series, *The Rise of the Sunbelt Cities* (vol. 14), may be of interest. After reviewing the conditions and potentials of winter cities in part two, the book turns to an analysis of issues and cases associated with the concept of transactional cities and transactional urbanization in part three. In part four, the contributors examine in more detail some of the developmental realities of industrial cities, both specifically and in general.

76. Linn, Johannes F. *Cities in the Developing World: Policies for Their Equitable and Efficient Growth.* New York: Oxford University Press, 1983. 230 p. OCLC 9043707.

The unprecedented rate of urban growth in developing nations has created massive new tasks for national and local policymakers. This study delineates the major problems of adapting to the growth of cities in developing countries, and it discusses policies to increase the efficiency and equity of urban development. The areas covered include urban employment, income redistribution, transport, housing, and social services. The study also evaluates the effectiveness of policy instruments such as public investment, pricing, taxation, and regulation. Written originally for the *World Development Report, 1979,* it has been published for wider dissemination of the information in it.

77. Marlin, John Tepper; Ness, Immanuel; and Collins, Stephen T. *Book of World City Rankings.* New York: Free Press, 1986. 604 p. OCLC 12695526.

The data and analysis in this book are intended to provide a general framework for the understanding of life in 105 world urban centers. Part one describes the environmental, demographic, economic, and service delivery data in each of the 105 world cities, grouped by country and region. Part two then compares all the cities on each indicator, and where comparative statistical data are not available, the text provides qualitative information on the most critical factors bearing on each city's social welfare, economic composition, and continuing development.

COMMODITIES

78. *Commodity Year Book.* New York: Commodity Research Bureau, 1939–. (Annual) OCLC 2259600.

This is considered to be the best single source for commodity information. Statistical tables of more than 110 commodities are arranged alphabetically by product. Information is given on supply, demand, consumption, prices, and export of raw and semifinished products. Numerous charts illustrate statistics. Each annual issue also contains feature studies to help the user project future price trends and recognize potentially profitable trading opportunities in selected commodities. *Statistical Abstract Service,* published three times a year by the same publisher, updates statistics in the yearbook.

79. Economist Intelligence Unit (Great Britain). *World Business Cycles.* London: Economist Newspaper, 1982. 191 p. OCLC 9086957.

This book provides a broad look at world business cycles and includes detailed information for eighty-four countries on gross domestic product and other related series during the period 1950–80. Information on world production is provided for thirty-four commodities. Also included is a long-term view of gross domestic product, and other series of interest, for the United Kingdom and the United States, during the period from the 1850s to 1980. The Economist Commodity Price Index is included for 1860 to 1980 as a guide to changes in commodity prices. The volume is divided into four main sections: "World Business Cycles 1950–80," taking a broad look at main items of economic interest; a long-term view, taking a look at various items of economic interest for the period 1850–80; "Countries 1950–80," which includes detailed figures for eighty-four countries; and "Commodities 1950–80," which includes detailed figures for thirty-four commodities. Altogether, it covers about eighty countries and over thirty commodities for a thirty-year period extending back to 1950 although in some instances it goes further back.

80. Economist Intelligence Unit (Great Britain). *World Commodity Outlook 1987: Industrial Raw Materials.* London, 1986. 120 p. OCLC 13574882.

This publication provides 120 pages of data analysis and forecasts on the world scene for industrial raw materials: nonferrous metals (copper, aluminum, tin, silver, zinc, lead, antimony); steel and its raw materials; alloying metals (nickel, chrome, tungsten, molybdenum, cobalt); fibres (cotton, wool, and jute); and rubber. After an extensive assessment of the world picture, individual products are examined, each with a one-page summary of world reserves, output, consumption, trade, and average prices. A detailed analysis of the present situation and future possibilities are given.

81. International Wheat Council (IWC). *World Wheat Statistics, 1985.* London, 1985. 111 p.

This is the thirty-first issue and includes data on wheat production, imports, exports, supplies and stocks, basic support levels, export and import prices, ocean freight rates, and wheat utilization in selected countries. Information is also given on trade, stocks, prices, world closing stocks, wheat consumption, and bread prices in selected counmtries. Most of the tables give a data series over a long period, ending with the crop year 1983–84, or estimates for 1984–85. World tables are shown under the three main economic groupings: Developed Countries, Centrally Planned Countries, and Developing Countries.

82. United Nations Conference on Trade and Development (UNCTAD). *UNCTAD Commodity Yearbook.* New York, 1987. 584 p. OCLC 11921262.

Headquarted in Geneva, this U.N. agency was established in 1964 primarily to promote international trade and formulate and implement principals and policies thereof. The *UNCTAD Commodity Yearbook* is the new title of the third edition of the *Yearbook of International Commodity Statistics.* As with the first and second editions, this one also provides disaggregated data at the world regional and country levels for trade in selected agricultural primary commodities and minerals, ores, and metals. Most of the tables cover the period 1972 to 1984. This publication does provide a comprehensive country-specific statistical series for a wide range of commodities covering the periods from thirteen to twenty-four years. It is indeed an excellent source for international commodity trade values, of exports and imports of merchandise, although the tables may not be easy for comprehension by lay people.

83. United Nations. Department of International Economic and Social Affairs. *Commodity Trade Statistics.* New York, 1949–. (Irregular)
Provides quarterly and annual data for countries in terms of the 625 subgroups of the Standard International Trade Classification (SITC). Data for each reporting country are published together. The data are shown in reporting country-by-commodity-by-partner-country order.

84. United Nations. Food and Agriculture Organization (FAO). *Commodity Review and Outlook: 1985–1986.* Rome, Italy, 1986. 132 p.
This highlights the world market developments for major agricultural commodities and commodity groups. It draws attention to events affecting developing countries both as exporters and importers. Each edition features a special article on commodity production, demand, and trade. Also available in French and Spanish.

85. United Nations. International Narcotics Control Board. *Statistics on Narcotic Drugs for 1984: Furnished by Governments in Accordance with the International Treaties.* New York, 1985. 106 p. OCLC 10947636.
Headquartered in Vienna and established in 1964, the task of this U.N. agency is to promote compliance by governments with the various drug control treaties. This publication provides information concerning the actual utilization of narcotic drugs. For purposes of comparison, statistics for the previous four years have been included in the tables. This document, read along with the publication *Estimated World Requirements of Narcotic Drugs* (in a given year), provides the proper perspective in understanding the production and consumption of narcotic drugs worldwide. It is trilingual: English, French, and Spanish.

86. World Bank. *Commodity Trade and Price Trends.* Distributed for the World Bank by the Johns Hopkins University Press, 1986. Vol. 38. 96 p. OCLC 15608940.
The purpose of this annual publication is to present factual information on the trade of countries and to provide eighty-four market price quotations for fifty-five commodities which figure importantly in international trade. It also contains a list of the economic classification of countries and regions used in this publication as well as a list of the United Nations Standard International Trade Classification codes covering the commodities listed in the trade tables. A selected set of general price indices that can be used as deflators and selected data on ocean freight rates are also provided. To facilitate comparability, all commodity prices are shown in a single currency, the U.S. dollar. In addition to the statistical and graphic presentation, an overview of the commodity price and trade trends are given. Parallel title and text are also in French and Spanish.

87. World Bank. *The Outlook for Primary Commodities: 1984 to 1995.* Washington, DC, 1984. 85 p. OCLC 11519065.
This volume is part of a five-volume report which reviews the market prospects for the major primary commodities exported by developing countries. Since 1980, this report has been published every two years. Volume one examines the movements in commodity prices over the past

two years and compares the forecasts made two years ago with prices realized in 1982 and 1983. Volume two covers the commodity specific discussions on the outlook for production, consumption, trade, and prices of food products and fertilizers up to the year 1995. Volume three presents the outlook for agricultural raw materials, volume four covers metals and minerals, and volume five presents the outlook for the energy commodities (oil, coal, and natural gas).

ECONOMIC ASSISTANCE

88. Cassen, Robert, et al, eds. *Rich Country Interests and Third Country Development.* New York: St. Martins Press, 1982. 369 p. OCLC 8669292.

This provides a good deal of straightforward informatiom about the attitudes and policies of the industrialized nations to the third world countries. Separate chapters examine broadly the individual countries and their historical, political, and other factors that influence their relations with the third world. There is a thirty-five-page statistical appendix of great value.

89. European Communities (EC). *EEC and the Third World: A Survey.* London: Hodder and Stoughton, 1981–. (Annual) OCLC 7470084.

This is published in association with the Overseas Development Institute and the Institute of Development Studies. The survey provides an annual record of and commentary on major developments in the European Community's economic relations with the third world. The first in this series deals with the Lome (capital of Togo, a former African colony) Covention, designed to provide a response to the varying needs of developing countries signatory to the convention. The principal aid and development policies of the European Community as a unit are carried out through the Lome Agreement. The agreement is with sixty ACP (African, Caribbean, and Pacific) countries. The second one in this series deals with hunger in the world. Beginning with the third one, each edition has an individual title.

The title for the third one is *The Atlantic Rift* (published 1983), and its central theme is the growing division between the EC and the U.S., regarding their policies toward the third world. The fourth one in this series is called *Renegotiating Lome*, and it contains a thorough examination of the Lome Institutions and discusses whether or not the convention has really developed trade links between the EC and the ACP signatory countries. Special attention is paid to the orientation of EC aid. *Survey 5* is titled *Pressure Groups, Policies, and Developments,* and it focuses on the activities of some of the key pressure groups and developing Non-Government Organizations (NGO). Although the topics covered by the survey vary, the common feature of it is the "Statistical Appendix" that illustrates key features of the EC-third world links.

90. Ghosh, Pradip K., ed. *Development Co-operation and Third World Development.* Westport, CT: Greenwood Press, 1984. 497 p. OCLC 10324861.

Like other volumes in the International Development Resource Books series, this one also consists of four parts. Part one consists of eleven previously published papers, mostly U.N. and OECD documents. Part two includes statistical information although there are statistical tables throughout the book. Part three contains an annotated bibliography, and part four is a directory of information sources.

91. Girling, Robert Henriques. *Multinational Institutions and the Third World: Management, Debt, and Trade Conflicts in the International Economic Order.* New York: Praeger, 1985. 212 p. OCLC 11468893.

As the problem of third world debt and the consequences of default loom higher on the international economic agenda, some coherent perspectives that bear on the actual and ideal roles of the multinational institutions are presented here. In a wide ranging analysis, the book demonstrates that the debt problem cannot be resolved without simultaneously addressing the restrictions on the third world exports and chronically poor export prices. Finally, countertrade is explored as an effective temporary solution to the debt problem with the potential to ensure balanced trade, promote South-South trade, and increase third world access to industrial markets.

92. Hewitt, Adrian. *Business Guide to World Aid Funds and Projects.* 2d ed. London: F. Pinter, 1983. 135 p. OCLC 11916432.

This gives comprehensive coverage of world aid flows including bilateral, multilateral, and voluntary aids.

93. Organization for Economic Cooperation and Development (OECD). *Aid from OPEC Countries: Efforts and Policies of the Members of OPEC and of the Aid Institutions Established by OPEC Countries.* Paris, 1983. 163 p. OCLC 9612341.

Formerly Organization for European Economic Cooperation, the OECD was formed in 1961. It is the principal economic oragnization of the industrialized countries of the North. Its establishing convention emphasizes the OECD's world role. It presently has twenty-four members including the United States, Canada, Japan, Australia, and New Zealand. Members are pledged to work together to promote economic growth, aid developing countries, and expand world trade. The headquarters are in Paris.

OPEC countries, except Venezuela, do not publish information on their aid activities. Based on the annual reports and additional information supplied by the Abu Dhabi Fund for Arab Economic Development, the Kuwait Fund for Arab Economic Development, the Saudi Fund for Development, the Venezuelan Investment Fund, as well as information from the Ministries of Finance of some of the OPEC member countries, this study summarizes OPEC aid. It also describes the programs of each country and each OPEC/Arab multilateral aid agency.

94. Organization for Economic Cooperation and Development (OECD). *Geographical Distribution of Financial Flows to Developing Countries.* Paris, 1969–. (Biennial, Annual) OCLC 7414431.

The 1982–85 edition, published in 1987, is subtitled "Disbursements, Committments, Economic Indicators"; and it is the seventh report in this series. This is unique in supplying data on the sources, volume, and terms of official aid receipts for 110 selected developing nations. It also gives the origin, type, and inflow of other external financial resources. Background economic data are also provided as perspective in interpreting the resource flow information for each country.

95. United Nations Conference on Trade and Development (UNCTAD). *Development and Recovery: The Realities of the New Interdependence Report.* By the Secretary General of the United Nations on Trade and Development to the Sixth Session of the Conference. New York, 1984. 60 p. OCLC 12420881.
This report is divided into four chapters as follows: (1) The World Economy in Crisis; (2) The Immediate Response: A Programme For Recovery; (3) The Long-Term Perspective: The Dynamics of the New Interdependence; and (4) The Adaptation of the Systems: Some Basic Elements. The periodic sessions of the conference have addressed themselves to a wide range of issues with particular emphasis on the needs of developing countries in the world economy. The developing countries now have an undoubted presence on the world economic scene. The health of their economies taken together is of much greater consequence to the world economy than ever before. This new interdependence and the action demanded are the focus of this report.

96. United Nations Conference on Trade and Development (UNCTAD). *Financial Solidarity for Development: Development Assistance from OPEC Members and Institutions to Other Developing Countries, 1977–1983: Report.* New York, 1985. 180 p. OCLC 13117206.
This is the fourth report on financial assisstance from OPEC members to other developing countries prepared by the UNCTAD Secretariat. It reviews the efforts made by OPEC to assisst other developing countries in their development efforts. It also analyzes the full range of aid flows to developing countries as also the growing financial cooperation among them. It reveals a widespread emphasis on the lower income developing countries in Africa and Asia, particularly the least developed category. The report also documents the activities of the Arab Monetary Fund (AMF) and the Arab Gulf Programme for the United Nations Development Organization (AGFUND).

97. United Nations. Director General for Development and International Economic Cooperation. *Towards the New International Economic Order.* New York, 1982. 73 p. OCLC 8353653.
This is subtitled "Analytical Report on Developments in the Field of International Economic Cooperation since the Sixth Special Session of the General Assembly." One of the principal conclusions that emerges from this study is that, in future efforts to establish the New International Economic Order, a decision-making process that is multisectoral in its coverage and universal in its participation is called for. The New International Economic Order is a concept, an offshoot, from the 1973 Conference of Non-Aligned Nations, aimed at fundamental restructuring of the world economy to benefit the South.

98. World Bank. *Abstracts of Current Studies.* Washington, DC, 1982–. OCLC 9038687.

It is aimed to broaden the understanding of the development process. These compilations provide a summary of ongoing work in the World Bank's Central Research Program. Short-term studies carried out by the bank's staff are not generally included. Also excluded are projects funded by loans and credits to member governments. Now, in its sixteenth year, the program covers a broad range of development-oriented issues in about sixty countries. The wide ranging topical interest of the research portfolio is a reflection of the types of policy advice and information that are sought by member countries and of the data requirements of the bank as a leading development institution.

ECONOMIC GEOGRAPHY

99. Crow, Ben, and Thomas, Alan. *Third World Atlas.* Milton Keynes, England: Open University Press, 1983. 72 p. OCLC 11218315.

It is not a conventional collection of maps. It introduces alternative ways of defining and mapping the third world and development. The atlas presents a variety of perspectives and explores how data can be presented and interpreted and how much reliance can be placed on it. It offers both historical and contemporary contexts discussing, for instance, Europe's colonization of Asia, Africa, and Latin America, and current issues such as indebtedness, multinational corporations, and women's work in developing economies. It provides important spatial and statistical dimensions to study the third world.

100. Dickenson, J. P., et al. *A Geography of the Third World.* London: Methuen, 1983. 283 p. OCLC 9413632.

In this textbook, the third world is set firmly in the wider context of the world economy. This presents a contemporary geography of the third world exploring systematic themes in the development process and examines spatial patterns of development and underdevelopment at various scales. The book concludes by summarizing that it offers geography an opportunity to put its theories and techniques to practical use in the understanding and solution of at least some of the problems of a large part of the earth and its population.

101. Dutt, Ashok K., and Geib, M. Margaret. *Atlas of South Asia.* Boulder, CO: Westview Press, 1987. 231 p. OCLC 14196316.

This atlas includes maps, figures, and narratives that provide a comprehensive coverage of economic, political, physical, historical, and cultural aspects of South Asia. India is given major focus with a secondary emphasis on Pakistan and Bangladesh. Sri Lanka, Nepal, and Bhutan are given shorter treatment. Although the maps are the main focus, the accompanying text explains and interprets the visual materials. Topics such as climate, physical features, and historical setting are examined for the subcontinent as a whole in the chapter on South Asia. In subsequent country chapters, economics, agriculture, industry, natural resources, trade, transportation, and demographic characteristics are dealt with.

102. Jumper, Sidney R.; Bell, Thomas L.; and Ralston, Bruce A. *Economic Growth and Disparaties: A World View.* Englewood Cliffs, NJ: Prentice-Hall, 1980. 472 p. OCLC 5675588.

This is an introduction to selected geographic dimensions of world economic activities. The basic emphasis is on differential characteristics of economic development and the striking contrasts that exist among people residing in the affluent and the poor nations of the world. Throughout the book, emphasis is given to an understanding of real world differences in levels of human dvelopment and in comprehending world economic issues.

103. Reitsma, H. A., and Kleinpenning, J. M. G. *The Third World in Perspective.* Totowa, NJ: Rowman & Allanheld, 1985. 420 p.

This is a well-written geography in which current economic, social, and political problems are examined. The problems of urban squatters, land reform, poverty, health care, refugees, overpopulation, and cultural conflict endemic to the third world are also covered. Two distinguished geographers use four analytical approaches—topical, regional, historical, and comparative—to analyze the problems of the third world. For developed nations to understand the variety and diversity of countries and regions lumped together as the third world, such a detailed account of the manner in which development processes have contributed to the distinguishing political, social, and economic characteristics of these countries is a big step. Prior to 1982, there was not a single English-language geography text that dealt specifically with the problems of underdevelopment. Such a text has, however, been available in Dutch since 1978. This book is based on the Dutch publication, *Profiel van de Derde Wereld* (Profile of the Third World).

ECONOMIC INDICATORS

104. Baldwin, Harriet. *The Development Data Book.* Washington, DC: World Bank, 1984. 33 p. OCLC 11629685.

This book presents statistics on 125 countries with populations of more than one million. The statistics relate to economic development and the changes it is bringing about in the world or, in other words, economic indicators. Because the world economy has become interdependent, economic development affects all countries. In order that people everywhere can understand more about economic development and about the differences in living conditions between developed and developing nations, World Bank has published this book to promote that understanding.

105. Moore, Geoffrey Hoyt, and Moore, Melita H. *International Economic Indicators: Sourcebook.* Westport, CT: Greenwood Press, 1985. 373 p. OCLC 11114228.

Although it is a sourcebook of economic indicators, a major part of it contains statistical information from these indicators which are useful in learning about the economic performance of the industrialized nations.

106. Organization for Economic Cooperation and Development (OECD). *Consumer Price Indices: Sources and Methods and Historical Statistics.* 2d ed. Paris, 1984. 143 p. OCLC 11313119.
The consumer price index (CPI) is an instrument designed to measure changes over time in the prices paid by households for the goods and services which they customarily purchase for consumption. The preliminary pages take up the basic concepts followed by a listing of CPI with its essential features for each member country including the U.S. The statistics supplied cover the period 1960 to 1983. It is bilingual: English and French.

107. Organization for Economic Cooperation and Development (OECD). *Indicators of Industrial Activity.* Paris, 1979–. (Quarterly).
This is the outcome of the merger of two former publications, *Short Term Economic Indicators for Manufacturing Industry,* and *Industrial Production: Quarterly Supplement to "Main Economic Indicators."* This publication is intended to provide an overall view of economic developments in different industries. It is divided into two sections, the first showing quantitative statistics and the second, qualitative business survey data. It is in English and French.

108. Organization for Economic Cooperation and Development (OECD). *Living Conditions in OECD Countries; A Compendium of Social Indicators.* Paris, 1986. 165 p. OCLC 13517459.
This book quantifies measures of well-being within the OECD countries in the areas of health, education, working life and leisure, and financial and personal security. Without doubt, this gives a general idea of living conditions in the OECD region.

109. Organization for Economic Cooperation and Development (OECD). *Main Economic Indicators: Historical Statistics: 1964–1983.* rev ed. Paris, 1984. 656 p. OCLC 11148413.
This volume is arranged in chapters by country. The tables cover the period 1964 to 1983, and they are followed by short notes describing some major characteristics of the series. Published sources are cited at the end of each chapter. This publication is a collection of international statistics on the economic developments of the OECD region for the past two decades and is based on the most up-to-date techniques of tabular and graphic presentation and is designed to provide at a glance a picture of the most recent changes in the economy of OECD countries. The indicators selected cover industrial production, construction, retail sales, labor, wages, prices, domestic and foreign finance, interest rates, trade, and payments. It also contains tabulation of international economic activities. It is bilingual: English and French.

110. Taylor, Charles Lewis, and Jodice, David A. *World Handbook of Political and Social Indicators.* 3d ed. New Haven, CT: Yale University Press, 1983. 2 vols. OCLC 9194705.
This book offers interesting comparative indicators including standard economic ones to review the countries of the world in terms of their political and social characteristics. Some of the topics covered are eco-

nomic structure, wealth, health, distribution of income, social relations, and education.

ENERGY

111. International Energy Agency (IEA). *Annual Oil and Gas Statistics and Main Historical Series, 1984–1985.* Paris, 1987. 419 p. (Annual)
The IEA was set up by the council of the OECD in 1974 to develop cooperation on energy questions among participating countries. The member countries, which include U.S. and Canada, signed an agreement on International Energy Program which has been effective since 1976. The program commits participating countries to share oil in emergencies and to strengthen their long-term cooperation in order to reduce dependence on the oil market.

The present publication is the twenty-fourth in this series. This volume contains comprehensive statistics on oil and natural gas based on annual submissions of OECD member countries including the U.S. and Canada. Figures in the summary balance are for the years 1973 to 1985. It is bilingual in English and French.

112. International Energy Agency (IEA). *Energy Policies and Programs of IEA Countries: 1985 Review.* Paris, 1986. 555 p. OCLC 14205988.
Its value lies not only in energy information it provides, but also in summary statistical information on economic performance of IEA countries (mostly OECD member countries). A companion and supplementary volume is *Energy Research Development and Demonstration in the IEA Countries* (OECD, 1985).

113. International Energy Agency (IEA). *Energy Statistics and Main Historical Series: 1983–1984.* Paris, 1986. 291 p.
This publication is intended mainly for those involved in analytical and policy work related to international energy issues. It provides detailed statistics on production, trade, and consumption for each source of energy in all OECD countries. Data have been taken from questionnaires completed by member countries and supplemented from national statistical publications or other reliable sources.

114. International Energy Agency (IEA). *World Energy Outlook.* Paris, 1982. 473 p. OCLC 8877225.
Different facets of the overall world energy picture are examined in detail. Likely effects of market forces and the direction of the economy under pressure from price, demand, and policy are quantified. This is the second such analysis, the first one being issued in 1977.

115. Organization for Economic Cooperation and Development (OECD). *Energy Statistics, 1983–1984.* Paris, 1986. 178 p.
This annual publication presents detailed statistics on production, trade, and consumption for each source of energy. Statistics cover a four-year period for all OECD countries and main regions. It is bilingual: English and French.

116. United Nations Conference on Trade and Development (UNCTAD). *Energy Supplies for Developing Countries: Issues in Transfer and Development of Technologies.* New York, 1980. 86 p. OCLC 7163930.

This contains a study of energy consumption, production, and trade in developing countries. This also analyzes the structure of the international market for technologies in the energy sector. The publication is divided into four parts. Part one aims at setting the problem in perspective by summarizing the energy situation in developing countries along with a global picture. Part two analyzes the structure of the international market for different energy technologies. Part three examines the experience of developing countries in the transfer and development of technology in the energy sector. Part four provides a general summary.

117. United Nations. Department of International Economic and Social Affairs. *The Energy Statistics Yearbook.* New York, 1984–. (Annual)

It commenced under the title *World Energy Supplies in Selected Years* with the 1951–54 edition (published 1957). The title then changed to *Yearbook of World Energy Statistics* with the 1979 edition (published 1981), and the latest change of title is the one noted at the beginning of the entry with the 1983 edition. The 1984 edition (published 1986) is the latest available. It is a comprehensive collection of international energy statistics. The principal objective of the yearbook is to provide a global framework of comparable data on long-term trends in the supply of mainly commercial primary and secondary forms of energy. Data for each type of fuel and aggregate data for the total mix of commercial fuels are shown for individual countries and are summarized into regional and world totals. Anyone interested in statistics prior to the year 1950 may consult *World Energy Supplies in Selected Years*, published by the same agency.

118. United Nations. Economic and Social Commission for Asia and the Pacific (ESCAP). *Energy in the ESCAP Region: Policies, Issues, and the Potential for Regional Cooperation.* Bangkok, Thailand, 1984. 179 p. OCLC 12098815.

This volume examines at some length the experience of China, Fiji, Hong Kong, Malaysia, Papua New Guinea, the Philippines, Singapore, and Thailand in energy management. The special emphasis of this study is on energy conservation and interfuel substitution. Statistical tables are provided.

119. United Nations. Economic Commission for Europe (ECE). *Annual Bulletin of Electric Energy Statistics for Europe.* New York, 1955–. (Annual) OCLC 1483422.

The purpose of this bulletin is to provide basic data on developments and trends in the field of electric energy in European countries, Canada, and the U.S. The data refer to the capacity of plants, production, consumption, supplies to consumers, consumption of fuels, and corresponding production of electric energy, trade, and international exchanges. This publication is purely statistical in character, and figures are given for the last four years. Titles and text are in English, French, and Russian. The 1984 volume (published in 1985) is the latest available.

120. United Nations. Statistical Office. *Energy Balances and Electricity Profiles 1984.* New York, 1986. 483 p. OCLC 15080323.
For more than thirty years, the U.N. has been publishing world energy data in the *Energy Statistics Yearbook* (formerly *Yearbook of World Energy Statistics*) where information on production, trade, stock, and consumption is presented on individual commodities for approximately 200 countries of the world. Through this publication, the U.N. reflects the shift in perspectives toward the demand structure of energy by adding overall energy balances and electricity profiles for developing countries.

121. World Energy Conference. *World Energy, Looking Ahead to 2020: Report.* New York: Published for the World Energy Conference by IPC Science and Technology Press, 1978. 274 p. OCLC 8110195.
This discusses the potential supply of energy from all primary energy sources, the impact of possible conservation measures, and likely energy demand scenarios for the period to 2020. The report is worldwide in scope and covers all nations of the world.

ENVIRONMENT

122. *The Global 2000 Report to the President: Entering the Twenty-First Century: A Report.* Washington, DC: U.S. Government Printing Office, 1980–81. 3 vols. OCLC 7281113.
This is a report prepared by the U.S. Council on Environmental Quality (a White House Agency) and the Department of State. The three volumes are subtitled as follows: volume one, "Summary Report"; volume two, "The Technical Report"; and volume three, "The Global 2000 Report to the President: Documentation on the Government's Global Sectoral Models, the Government's 'Global Model.'" This is a comprehensive report on the environment touching on all aspects of natural resources and their availability. It also contains chapters on population, gross national product, climate, technology, food, fisheries, forestry, water, energy, and minerals. It also provides an excellent overview for questions on future food consumption and supply, water availability, energy demand, pollutants, and the demand for individual materials. *Global 2000* received an extraordinarily wide circulation, and it has influenced crucial government policies. Even before the report was completed, President Carter had discussed its conclusions with other world leaders at an economic summit held in Italy. In his farewell address, he also referred to the subject of *Global 2000* as one of the three most important problems facing the American people (the other two being arms control and human rights). The press gave the report enormous attention.

123. Organization for Economic Cooperation and Development (OECD). *OECD Environmmental Data: Compendium, 1985.* Paris, 1985. 297 p.
Being concerned with the qualitative and quantitative aspects of economic growth, OECD presents a core set of comparable environmental information for member countries. This is a compendium of statistical data concerning the state of the environment in OECD countries. It supple-

ments the highly readable OECD publication, *The State of the Environment, 1985.* This pulication is bilingual in English and French.

124. Organization for Economic Cooperation and Development (OECD). *The State of the Environment.* Paris, 1985. 271 p. OCLC 13006262.
It reviews progress achieved since the first OECD report in 1979. This second report examines the pressures on the environment from agriculture, energy, industry, and transport activities as well as the responses of the public, of enterprises, and of government to these pressures. A useful statistical companion volume is *OECD Environmental Data: Compendium, 1985.*

125. Simon, Julian L., and Kahn, Herman, ed. *The Resourceful Earth: A Response to Global 2000.* London: Basil Blackwell, 1984. 585 p. OCLC 10996292.
This is a response to, and highly critical of, *Global Report to the President.* It is a compendium of independent studies of many of the topics dealt with by *Global 2000.* It is intended to be an assessment of the trends together with an analysis of what the trends portend for the future. The general point of view that underlies it is that in the long run, both before and also subsequent to the year 2000, the economic growth will continue. It is implied that there is no reason to expect stagnation or a lower percentage rate growth for the least developed countries in the future compared to the past. This expectation is quite unlike the one stated by *Global 2000.*

126. United Nations. Department of International Economic and Social Affairs. *Directory of Environment Statistics.* New York, 1983. 305 p. OCLC 10933388.
This provides a standard inventory against which data availability and country practices and plans in the field of environment statistics can be assessed. The directory covers U.N. member states only, and data were not available for Benin, Bhutan, Comoros, Dominica, Guinea, Sao Tome, Principe, and Suriname. Countries are listed in alphabetical order.

EXTERNAL DEBT

127. Claudon, Michael P., ed. *World Debt Crisis: International Lending on Trial.* Cambridge, MA: Ballinger Publishing Co, 1986. 298 p. OCLC 12343303.
It is a collection of essays that grew out of the 1984 Middlebury College Conference dealing with third world debt. The conference has been described to be "extraordinarily well planned, innovative, rounded, and complete," and all of these are evident in the book itself. It is divided into four parts. The opening part provides a historical touchstone for the rest of the book. Herein is a detailed description of the debt crisis's historical antecedents and a glimpse of what the future portends for this problem. Part two discusses the U.S. Federal Reserve System's view and Wall Street's reaction to the handling of the debt crisis. Part three examines the international financial institution's view of the crisis and how it was dealt

with. The global debt crisis is also assessed from the IMF's perspective. Part four deals mainly with the question of why the debt crisis is concentrated in Latin America. The book has much statistical information of value in comprehending the international debt problem.

128. Cline, William R. *The International Debt and the Stability of the World Economy.* Washington, DC: Institute for International Economics, 1983. 134 p. OCLC 9663537.

This is the shorter and somewhat less technical version of the author's *International Debt: Systematic Risk and Policy Response* (published in 1984). This publication presents a comprehensive analysis of the world debt crisis. In section one, the origins of the debt problem are analyzed. Section two examines the potential risk to industrial country economies and financial systems posed by the debt of developing and eastern European countries. It also reviews the debt packages orchestrated by the IMF, the U.S. government, and others. Section three is a projection of the debt and balance of payments of the large debtor countries, and herein the level of world economic growth plays a large role. Section four analyzes the dynamics of involuntary lending and the technical aspects of debt rescheduling. Section five examines the link and adequacy of banking institutions to debt. In section six the projections of this study are matched against prospective levels of international financing. Section seven discusses the plans that have been proposed as a solution to the debt problem. The policy conclusions are summarized in section eight. In short, it is a factual, analytical, and thorough appraisal of the global debt problem.

129. Hardy, Chandra S. *Rescheduling Developing Country Debts, 1956–1981.* Washington, DC: Overseas Development Council, 1982. 74 p.

This provides an analysis of the economic circumstances of ten countries (Argentina, Brazil, Chile, Ghana, India, Indonesia, Pakistan, Peru, Turkey, and Zaire) during the five-year period prior to their first debt rescheduling and the consequences. The conclusion of this offers suggestions for reform of debt rescheduling procedures. A prerequisite to such reform is change in attitudes to debt relief including recognition of rescheduling as a normal feature of borrowing and lending in uncertain times.

130. Lewis, John P., and Kallab, Valeriana, ed. *U.S. Foreign Policy and the Third World: Agenda, 1983.* New York: Praeger, 1983. 293 p.

The book focuses on globalism, regionalism, interdependence, third world interdependence in particular, and the debt crisis of developing countries. The program advocated in this book to recapture the benefits of interdependence is also believed to promote and sustain the U.S. economic recovery. A very carefully drawn out seven-part statistical appendix of 128 pages is a most useful feature of the book as can be seen from the breakdown which follows: Indicators of U.S.–Third World Interdependence; World Economic Indicators; Indicators of Economic and Social Development; Food and Energy; World Trade; World Military Expenditures; and Financial Flows.

131. Nunnenkamp, Peter. *The International Debt Crisis of the Third World: Causes and Consequences for the World Economy.* New York: St. Martin's Press, 1986. 205 p. OCLC 11755983.

The third world's economic difficulties became a major issue of public debate in industrialized countries because of the widespread fear that these could adversely affect the economic well-being of the latter. This book discusses the causes, consequences, and solutions. It presents forty-five statistical tables of great informational value.

132. Organization for Economic Cooperation and Development (OECD). *Financial and External Debt of Developing Countries: 1985 Survey.* Paris, 1986. 235 p. OCLC 14369621.

This survey presents the latest information on financial resource flows to developing countries and their external indebtedness over the 1975–85 period. Statistical presentations include tables of aggregate resource flows and debt by main economic groups and selected countries as well as gives detailed information on total debt and debt service of each developing country for the period 1975 through 1984.

133. Sanderson, Warren C. *How Should Developing Countries Adjust to External Shocks in the 1980's.* Washington, DC: World Bank, 1985. 98 p.

This reviews the quantitative relationship between external shocks (primarily because of adverse export and import prices), economic policies, and performance across a sample of developing countries. Prepared as a background report for the *World Development Report 1984,* it reviews two types of studies. The first consists of cross-country comparative studies of the shock-policy-adjustment relationship. The second is the quantitative modeling of individual economies. This work provides an indication of some important interactions between shocks, policy, and performance.

134. Smith, Gordon W., and Cuddington, John T., ed. *International Debt and the Developing Countries.* Washington, DC: World Bank, 1985. 339 p. OCLC 11622331.

The book is a blend of microeconomic theories of international borrowing and lending along with country experience. The case studies that may be of general interest are Argentina, Brazil, Chile, Korea, and Mexico.

135. World Bank. *Debt and the Developing World: Current Trends and Prospects.* Washington, DC, 1984. Vol. 32. 26 p. OCLC 10348728.

This is an abridged version of the 1983–84 edition of the *World Debt Tables.* It contains statistical tables showing the medium-term and long-term external debt of 103 countries. This volume contains data for public and publicly guaranteed debt augmented by information on private non-guaranteed debt and major economic aggregates and by indicators that are used in analysis of debt and credit worthiness. In addition to the regional summaries and individual country tables, tabulations are shown for 102 countries (i.e., all countries except Hungary) and for groupings by income levels.

136. World Bank. *Developing Country Debt: Implementing the Consensus.* Washington, DC, 1987. 29 p. OCLC 15224196.

This is an abridged version of the 1986–87 edition of *World Debt Tables.* This gives an overview and summary tables from the above and contains statistical tables showing the external debt of 109 developing countries. Data are provided for eight years: 1970, 1975, and 1980 through 1985. The report shows that, while outstanding debt has shown little growth in the past year, two groups of countries have been adversely affected: highly indebted middle-income countries and low income African countries.

137. World Bank. *World Debt Tables: External Debt of Developing Countries, 1986–87 Edition.* Washington, DC, 1987. 493 p.

This annual report contains a compilation of data on the external public and publicly guaranteed debt of 109 developing countries. It presents statistical tables by country for long- and short-term debt and the use of IMF credit. It gives the aggregate position of all countries, major borrowers, and seventeen highly indebted borrowers. It also outlines characteristics of the debt situation. Furthermore, it includes for each country a set of four charts depicting debt stocks and associated indicators as well as flows of debt service and associated debt-service ratios.

FOOD

138. Organization for Economic Cooperation and Development (OECD). *Food Consumption Statistics: 1973–1982.* Paris, 1985. 564 p. OCLC 12430465.

This is the seventh volume in this series. It includes data relating to each year of the 1973 to 1982 period. The first volume for the year 1968 covered the period 1964–66. The 1970 volume covered 1960–68; the 1973 volume covered 1955–71; the 1975 volume covered 1955–73; the 1978 volume covered 1970–75; and the 1981 volume covered the years 1964–78. The food balance sheets are shown country by country, and the list covers all OECD member countries except Greece, Iceland, and Yugoslavia.

139. United Nations. Food and Agriculture Organization (FAO). *Agriculture: Toward 2000.* Rome, Italy, 1981. 134+ p. OCLC 8846113.

Portrays desperate situations in developing countries regarding demand for food and agricultural products. Presents statistical information along with qualitative analysis of statistical data. This is the revised and abbreviated version of a first provisional report presented to the 1979 FAO conference.

140. United Nations. Food and Agriculture Organization (FAO). *Food Aid in Figures, 1985.* Rome, Italy, 1986. 118 p. (Annual) OCLC 14372733.

The FAO continously monitors food aid flows and developments and publishes relevant up-to-date information in its monthly, *Food Outlook Reports,* and the quarterly, *Food Aid Bulletin.* The annual *Food Aid in Figures* complements these two publications by providing further details on food aid flows by donors, recipients, and commodities and by covering a longer time period. This is a trilingual publication: English, French, and Spanish.

141. United Nations. Food and Agriculture Organization (FAO). *Food Balance Sheets: 1979–81 Average.* Rome, Italy, 1984. 272 p. OCLC 12174659.

The food balances reflect the best available information on the food situation prevailing in the individual countries during the years mentioned. The presentation also allows for intercountry comparisons of dietary and trade patterns. In addition to the food balance sheets for individual countries, a table is included showing daily per capita food supplies in terms of calories, protein, and fat for the world, continents, regions, and economic classes. In 1949, food balance sheets were published for forty-one countries, the 1984 publication covers 146 countries.

142. United Nations. Food and Agriculture Organization (FAO). *The State of Food and Agriculture.* Rome, Italy, 1957?–. 73 p. OCLC 14704088.

This is a world review of factors affecting progress in food and agriculture in developing countries, state of natural resources, and the human environment for food and agriculture. In addition to the usual review of the recent world food and agricultural situation, each issue since 1957 has included one or more special studies of problems of long-term interest. The 1985 issue is the mid-decade (i.e., midpoint of the Third U.N. Development decade) review of food and agriculture. This is a trilingual publication: English, French and Spanish.

143. United Nations. Food and Agriculture Organization (FAO). *The World Meat Economy in Figures.* Rome, Italy, 1985. 192 p. OCLC 13665506.

It contains worldwide statistical information on production, trade, and consumption of the main types of meat (i.e., bovine, sheep, goat, pig, and poultry meat). Information of minor meats is not shown separately but is included in the figures for total meat. Meat is a major item in international agricultural trade, notwithstanding the low proportion of production which enters world trade. This is a trilingual publication: English, French, and Spanish.

HOUSING

144. United Nations. Department of International Economic and Social Affairs. *Compendium of Human Settlement Statistics, 1983.* New York, 1985. 541 p.

This publication is intended to serve as a statistical foundation for the global situation on settlements. This replaces the former *Compendium of Housing Statistics* and is to be issued five times per year. The statistics in this publication are organized into four general areas: (1) population; (2) land use; (3) housing; and (4) infrastructure and services. It covers statistics for 211 countries or areas and 196 cities. Most tables have been prepared mainly from data received in response to a human settlements statistics questionnaire circulated by the U.N. Statistical Office in 1982–83 or obtained from official publications. It is in English and French.

145. United Nations. Department of International Economic and Social Affairs. *Global Review of Human Settlements.* New York: Pergamon Press, 1976. OCLC 2383651.

This is prepared by the Statistical Office of the above department with the cooperation and assisstance from the Center for Housing, Building, and Planning of the same department, the ILO, WHO, FAO, and the International Statistical Institute. The data contained in this publication provide insights into conditions of living in human settlements and analyze population characteristics, extent and utilization of land area, rates of new construction, relative levels of investment devoted to housing, and community facilities and measures to monitor or control environment pollution.

146. United Nations. Economic Commission for Europe (ECE). *Relationship between Housing and the National Economy.* Prepared by the Research Institute for Building and Architecture (VUVA), Czechoslovakia. New York, 1985. 60 p. OCLC 15628812.

Subtitled "Synthesis Report on the Seminar Held in Prague (Czechoslovakia) 10–14 May, 1982," this study is a pioneer effort in demonstrating the role housing plays in the national economy. The relationship between housing production and consumption on the one hand and socioeconomic development on the other had never been studied in detail. Chapter one summarizes main features of the recent economic developments in the ECE region and basic changes taking place in the sphere of housing.

INDUSTRIES

147. Leontief, Wassily, et al. *The Future of Nonfuel Minerals in the U.S. and World Economy: Input-Output Projections, 1980–2030.* Lexington, MA: Lexington Books, 1983. 454 p. OCLC 9323009.

The need to improve the understanding of the role of materials in any economy, especially its effects on sectors and industry, and issues raised by growing international interdependence cannot be overemphasized. This study advances the understanding of shifts in the supply and demand for principal mineral resources under conditions of economic growth and technological advance. Nearly all aspects of changes in economic activity are addressed in this book. In addition, worldwide demographic, developmental, environmental, and political issues that affect the future position of the nonfuel minerals in the U.S. and in the world economy are covered. Part one concentrates on the current uses and sources of supply of twenty-six nonfuel minerals. Part two describes the use of each of the twenty-six minerals in the global context. Chapter seven, in particular, integrates the U.S. economy into the wider framework of the world economy and incorporates the current description and projection of the future levels of global consumption and production, region by region.

148. Organization for Economic Cooperation and Development (OECD). *Industrial Structure Statistics, 1983.* Paris, 1985. 136 p. OCLC 10810904.

Prepared by the Directorate for Science, Technology, and Industry of the OECD, this is the second issue of this publication. The book is divided into four parts. The first covers industrial statistics and exports and imports by industry. Part two deals with disaggregated national data by industry. Parts three and four include currency abbreviations and definitions. This is in English and French.

149. Organization for Economic Cooperation and Development (OECD). *Industry in Transition: Experience of the 70's and Prospects for the 80's.* Paris, 1983. 236 p.

This study deals with four subjects: the industrialization of developing countries, the trend of world demand, the pattern of investment, and the energy situation. According to the study, the changes in member countries' industrial structures and their ongoing adaptation to the economic, industrial and trade environment result from the interaction of many different forces. The study also points out that influences that have changed the industrial structures of member countries in recent years will continue through the foreseeable future. In examining how industry adapts to these changes, this report underlines the need for governments to reduce the present uncertainties about their own strategies and to encourage entrepreneurship.

150. United Nations. Department of International Economic and Social Affairs. *Construction Statistics Yearbook.* New York, 1984–. (Annual) OCLC 11938670.

The first issue in this series was entitled *Yearbook of Construction Statistics, 1963–72,* and it continued this title until 1981. Beginning 1982, it was simply called *Construction Statistics,* and beginning with the 1984 volume, it was titled *Construction Statistics Yearbook.* This publication is an annual, worldwide compilation of statistics on construction. It is divided into two parts: the first part contains the basic data for each country in the form of separate country chapters; the second part shows international tables on dwelling construction and on the index numbers of construction activity. The statistics are, in general, for a ten-year period. As soon as the data are assembled for a complete year, they are published in the yearbook in about two years.

151. United Nations. Department of International Economic and Social Affairs. *Industrial Statistics Yearbook.* New York, 1982–. (Annual) OCLC 12067944.

It continues *Yearbook of Industrial Statistics,* and it retained this title for the years 1974 to 1981. However, for the twenty-three years (1950 to 1973) preceding it, it was called *The Growth of World Industry.* This publication is designed to meet both the general demand for information of this kind and the special requirement of the U.N., particularly the UNIDO and other related international bodies. The *Industrial Statistics Yearbook* consists of two volumes: volume one, "General Industrial Statistics," and volume two, "Commodity Production Data." Volume one covers over 100 countries. The following are some of the items included for each branch of the industry: number of establishments; number of employees;

wages and salaries of employees; quantity of electricity consumed; gross output at current prices; cost of goods; services; materials and energy consumed; gross fixed capital formation; value of stocks; and index numbers of industrial production. In addition, special tables are included on indexes of industrial production and employment by branches of activity for the world and major regions. Volume two presents internationally comparable information on the production of more than 500 industrial commodities and for about 200 countries and areas including all major developed countries. The 1984 edition covers the five-year period from 1980 through 1984.

152. United Nations. Economic Commission for Europe (ECE). *Annual Review of Engineering Industries and Automation, 1983–84.* 2 vols. New York, 1985. (Annual)

Some ten years ago, ECE issued a publication entitled *The Role and Place of Engineering Industries in National and World Economies,* which was accompanied by extensive statistical material which was periodically brought up to date. Since 1981, the statistical updatings are being done on an annual basis under the above title. The present annual review consists of two volumes. The first one comprises the analytical material, and the second one contains the statistical annex. Volume one is arranged into four chapters but only chapters one and three may be of general interest. Chapter one deals with general economic developments in the region during the period 1983–84 in addition to covering engineering industries. Chapter three analyzes trends and developments in international trade in engineering products in 1983–84.

153. United Nations. Economic Commission for Europe (ECE). *East-West Industrial Cooperation.* New York, 1979. 122 p. OCLC 6011547.

This reviews the main developments in industrial cooperation which have taken place in the ECE region since the early 1970s. In addition to providing a framework for analyzing what was then a comparatively new form of East-West economic relations, the report analyzes the growth, forms, and motives of industrial cooperation as well as the advantages and problems associated with its development.

154. United Nations. Economic Commission for Europe (ECE). *Statistics of World Trade in Steel.* New York, 1961–. (Annual) OCLC 5328104.

This provides data on exports of semifinished and finished steel products from European and other steel exporting countries in the world. The preface, in recent editions, has been in English, French, and Russian. The publication is essentially bilingual: English and French.

155. United Nations. Economic Commission for Europe (ECE). *The Steel Market in 1984.* New York, 1985. 140+ p. OCLC 14106180.

The ECE has published annual reviews of the steel market since 1953. The above is the thirty-second publication, analyzes international and national developments, and is preceded by a summary. The part dealing with national developments contains statistical information which is preceded by a review of the trends in steel demand, supply, and prices. The annex to the review consists of statistical tables for international comparison of the principal trends.

156. United Nations. Industrial Development Organization (UNIDO). *Handbook of Industrial Statistics.* Vienna, Austria, 1986. 444 p. OCLC 15554626.

UNIDO became a specialized agency of the U.N. system in 1986. Since its origin in 1966, it had been an autonomous organization within the U.N. Secretariat. Its purpose is primarily to encourage and extend assisstance to the developing countries for the development, expansion, and moderniza- tion of their industries. Since 1975, special attention has been given to efforts aimed at raising the share of developing countries in world manu- facturing production.

This handbook provides a statistical analysis of major structural trends in seventy developing and developed countries. It also provides indicators relevant to drawing international comparisons of the process of industrialization. It includes patterns of consumption, industrial growth, the composition of net output in manufacturing, and export performance in key industries. Although it relies largely on available data (such as in *Commodity Trade Statistics, Yearbook of Industrial Statistics,* and *Year- book of International Trade Statistics*), it is original in two ways. First, the basic data accumulated have been combined to form indicators such as ratios, growth rates, indices, and rank orderings which facilitate compari- son. Second, many of the indicators presented are derived from estimates made by UNIDO to supplement data missing from the traditional sources.

157. United Nations Industrial Development Organization (UNIDO). *Industrial Development Survey.* New York, 1981–. (Biennial) OCLC 8036229.

It was originally issued in 1967 as a document for the International Symposium on Industrial Development held in Athens in 1967 and issued annually through the midseventies and biennially since 1981. The central theme of this publication is restructuring world industry, which is a primary objective of UNIDO. The annual volumes are generally divided into five parts as follows: (1) Restructuring World Industry—New Dimen- sions and Prospects; (2) The Export Performance of the Developing Coun- tries; (3) Restructuring World Industry—Trends and Prospects; (4) Energy Requirements in the Manufacturing Sector; and (5) The Trans-National Corporation as an Agent for Industrial Restructuring. The book has about 100 statistical tables.

158. United Nations. Industrial Development Organization (UNIDO). *Industry and Development: Global Report, 1986.* New York, 1985. 330 p. OCLC 12277622.

In addition to providing an analysis of the current situation by region, it gives a short-term forecast for 1986 and 1987 of the level of output in twenty-eight branches of industry in 150 countries. One of the main purposes of this publication is to provide an annual review of the current situation and immediate prospects of industrialization in developing coun- tries.

159. United Nations. Industrial Development Organization (UNIDO). *Industry in the 1980s: Structural Change and Interdependence.* Vienna, Austria, 1985. 228 p. OCLC 13098450.

This reviews the recent trends in the fields of industry that have particular relevance to global developments and analyzes various aspects of industrial interdependence in the context of that pattern. Some of the chapters are highlighted below. Chapter two is entitled "The Changing Map of the World Industry," and it begins with a brief account of recent changes in the global distribution of industrial activity. Chapter four touches on one of the most important objectives of industrialization, namely, increasing the availability of basic manufactures. Chapter ten begins with an analysis of the development of new industrially processed food products. From product development and technological advances, the chapter turns to the growing standardization in patterns of food consumption and production. The book has over eighty statistical tables.

160. United Nations. Industrial Development Organization (UNIDO). *International Comparative Advantage in Manufacturing: Changing Profiles of Resources and Trade.* Vienna, Austria, 1986. 226 p. OCLC 15548616.

The purpose of this publication is to provide the formulators of industrial and economic policies with empirical findings concerning international comparative advantage in manufacturing. The publication is based on data for all manufacturing activities in a wide range of countries between the early 1960s and the early 1980s. The statistical description comprises data on patterns of revealed comparative advantage and their changes between the early 1970s and the early 1980s, and the data are presented in the form of tables of trade manufactures and graphics of industry profiles. The summary is in French and Spanish.

161. United Nations. Industrial Development Organization (UNIDO). *World Industry since 1960: Progress and Prospects.* New York, 1979. OCLC 5238249.

This is a special issue of the Industrial Development Survey for the Third General Conference of UNIDO held in New Delhi, India, in 1980. This is an authoritative analysis of basic trends in the major areas of industry. The study evaluates the implications of the changing relationship between the developed and the developing nations. The extensive documentation and statistical data provide the basis for an outlook for future developments of world industry. This survey is published biennially in English, French, Russian, and Spanish as an integral part of the work program of UNIDO.

162. World Intellectual Property Organization (WIPO). *100 Years of Industrial Property Statistics.* Geneva, Switzerland, 1983. 245 p. OCLC 11290902.

As one of the specialized agencies of the U.N., the purpose and function of WIPO is to promote protection of intellectual property, inventions, copyrights, and access to patented technology. The publication is subtitled Synoptic Tables on Patents, Trademarks, Designs, Utility Models, and Plant Varieties, 1883–1982. This gives a worldwide coverage of industrial property statistics for the last 100 years. Parallel title and table of contents are in French.

LABOR SUPPLY

163. Gunatilleke, Godfrey, ed. *Migration of Asian Workers to the Arab World.* Tokyo, Japan: United Nations University, 1986. 358 p. OCLC 15073151.

In 1972, the U.N. General Assembly decided to establish an international university as an autonomous body of the assembly to be known as the United Nations University (UNU). This was to be a system of academic institutions consisting of affiliated institutions integrated into the world university community and devoted primarily to action-oriented research into the global problems of human survival.

In 1983, the UNU launched a project on the Global Impact of Human Migration with a major focus on migration caused by uneven industrialization in different countries and regions of the world. The first phase of the project was a state-of-the-art survey on migrant workers to the Arab world from seven countries (Bangladesh, India, Pakistan, Sri Lanka, Republic of Korea, the Philippines, and Thailand). The survey was conducted in a comparative framework to cover common problems of migration, both for the workers and for the government agencies concerned. This provides useful data and anlaysis on this problem along with some recommendations appropriate to each national situation.

164. International Labor Organization (ILO). *Bulletin of Labor Statistics.* Geneva, Switzerland, 1965–. (Quarterly) OCLC 1537758.

This provides general labor data on employment, unemployment, hours worked, wages, and consumer prices. These are compiled annually into the *Yearbook of Labor Statistics* which is also supplemented by this quarterly. Data in it are organized by continent and then by country. Monthly, quarterly, or semiannually, data are given for the last four years along with the annual statistics whenever possible. Eight supplements are issued annually to update figures in the quarterly bulletin. The interim supplements are in English, French, and Spanish.

165. International Labor Organization (ILO). *Labour Force Estimates and Projections, 1950–2000.* 2d ed. Geneva, Switzerland, 1977. 6 vols.

This edition supercedes data in a similar six-volume publication entitled *Labour Force Projections, 1965–1985* (1st ed., 1971). The six volumes in the current edition are volume one, Asia (155 p.); volume two, Africa (156 p.); volume three, Latin America (130 p.); volume four, Europe, North America, Oceania, and U.S.S.R. (135 p.); volume five, World Summary (135 p.); and volume six, Methodology (159 p.). Volumes one to five present data on population, the labor force, and labor force activity rates by sex and age group; and the data represent a comprehensive and consistent set of data for all countries, territories, regions, and major areas of the world.

166. International Labor Organization (ILO). *World Labor Report: Employment Incomes, Social Protection, New Information Technology.* Geneva, Switzerland, 1984. 215 p. OCLC 11370328.

The statistical annex in it presents international data on the structure of the economically active population, income distribution in selected countries, and the cost of social security. There are some fifty statistical tables and ten graphs, and almost every chapter contains specially displayed summaries and notes. The above publication, together with its second volume, subtitled *Labor Relations, International Labor Standards, Training, Conditions of Work, Women at Work* (published 1985), gives an overview of the main labor issues in the world. The third volume of this report, yet to be published, will concentrate on the question of pay.

167. McKersie, Robert B., and Sengenberger, Warner. *Job Losses in Major Industries.* Paris: OECD, 1983. 125 p.

Industrial societies continually face structural change. Recent years have seen extensive restructuring in certain economic sectors under the individual or combined effects of declining demand, technical change, and changing trade patterns. Many basic sectors (iron and steel, shipbuilding, textiles, and the motor industry) have been facing severe recession and are engaged in far-reaching conversion entailing massive job elimination. This report deals with the large-scale dislocations of employment in these sectors in a number of OECD countries. It describes their significance and the consequences, economic and other, for the workers, communities, and regions affected. It also discusses the structural changes which have led to these situations and the range of national and industrial strategies applied to respond to them. But the bulk of the report is devoted to a detailed analysis of intergrative strategies and conversion programs that seek to reconcile capital mobility with labor protection.

168. Organization for Economic Cooperation and Development (OECD). *Labour Force Statistics.* Paris, 1961–. (Annual) OCLC 2813674.

This yearbook presents annual statistics on the population and labor force of all member countries. This publication is prepared in the second quarter of each year and contains historical time series of the evolution of the population and the labor force for the twenty-four member countries. The first part of the yearbook consists of general tables illustrated by charts and graphs giving the major labor force aggregates with a breakdown by broad economic sectors. The second part contains country tables giving detailed statistics on the following main topics: population; major components of the labor force; civilian emolyment; and employment in manufacturing. The third part contains time series for participation rates and unemployment rates by age and sex for fifteen member countries. Since August 1975, the *Quarterly Labor Force Statistics* has been published in order to release most recent information as a supplement.

169. Organization for Economic Cooperation and Development (OECD). *OECD Employment Outlook.* Paris, 1985. 141 p. OCLC 11357526.

Recent labor market trends emphasize major differences in the job creating capabilities of different regions within the OECD area. Employment growth in the U.S. has been relatively strong, but the European economies are still facing rising unemployment. This report surveys current labor market trends and examines key developments.

170. Serageldin, Ismael, et al. *Manpower and International Labor Migration in the Middle East and North America.* New York: Published for the World Bank by Oxford University Press, 1983. 138 p. OCLC 8928417.

The book is a shortened version of the more detailed results and conclusions of a World Bank research project on "International Labor Migration and Manpower in the Middle East and North Africa from 1975–1976" and presents a wealth of information about the region. Having established regional trends, the book proceeds to detail qualitative aspects of the impacts of migration, with the use of a wide range of economic, labor market, and educational data brought together by projections. In short, the book identifies basic trends in economic and labor markets to stimulate thought over directions for policy and to indicate strategies and qualitative judgments.

NATIONAL INCOME

171. Kravis, Irving B., et al. *World Product and Income: International Comparisons of Real Gross Product.* Baltimore, MD: Published for the World Bank by the Johns Hopkins University Press, 1982. 388 p. OCLC 7814442.

This has been produced by the U.N. Statistical Office and the World Bank. This volume reports on the third phase of the U.N. International Comparison Project (ICP). The main results provide comparisons of real gross domestic product per capita for thirty-four countries in 1975. These new 1975 benchmark estimates considerably expand the phase one set covering six countries in 1967 and ten countries in 1970, and the phase two set covering six additional countries in 1970 and all sixteen in 1973.

172. Organization for Economic Cooperation and Development (OECD). *Latest Information on National Accounts of Developing Countries.* Paris, 1969–. OCLC 5805834.

This provides national accounts estimates of developing countries including summary tables on the growth of real product, population, and real product per capita by continent and by region. Also interesting is the classification of developing countries by various alternative characteristics including their per capita income, their dependency on oil, and their economic structure. When this series was started in the late 1960s, it had two main purposes: to bring together in a readily accessible form the national accounts estimates of developing countries that were then available only in widely scattered sources, and to provide details on the actual meaning and quality of the estimates shown. The 1986 volume contains five principal summary tables, each presenting information by continent, region, and country. The first table shows average annual growth rates of real product, population, and real product per capita for the ten-year periods of 1964–74 and 1974–84. Another table shows indices of real product for the years between 1970 and 1984, and still another gives percentage changes of real product for each year from 1970 to 1984. The fourth table comprises the basic data established for the two base years 1968 and 1981; the final table shows average annual growth rates of implicit prices of product for the following five-year periods: 1964–69,

1969–74, 1974–79, and 1979–84. Graphs of indices of real products are also shown. It is bilingual: English and French.

173. Organization for Economic Cooperation and Development (OECD). *National Account Statistics.* Paris, 1966?–. (Annual)
Title varies. Initially, it was entitled *National Accounts of OECD Countries,* and later it was called *National Accounts.* This is a two-volume work that provides detailed data, graphs, and comparisons on national income and expenditure and its various components for all member countries. The first volume gives for each country the main aggregates over a period of up to twenty years and comparative tables for twenty-five countries. Volume two contains detailed tables for national accounts for about the same period by country and for all the member countries including the U.S. Also included is gross domestic product by kind of activity and consumption expenditures. There is a *Quarterly National Accounts* providing the latest figures.

174. United Nations. Department of International Economic and Social Affairs. *National Accounts Statistics: Analysis of Main Aggregates.* New York, 1985–. (Annual) OCLC 12260297.
This was previously issued as *Yearbook of National Accounts Statistics.* The present publication actually replaces volume two—*International Tables*—and like that volume, it presents in the form of analytical tables a summary of the main national accounts aggregates. This is extracted from *National Accounts Statistics: Main Aggregates and Detailed Tables.*

175. United Nations. Department of International Economic and Social Affairs. *National Accounts Statistics: Compendium of Income Distribution Statistics.* New York, 1985. 552 p. OCLC 13712378.
It is volume seventy-nine in the department's Statistical Papers Series M, but it is, in fact, the first one in a projected series covering income distribution and household sector statistics. Future publications are intended to be published every three to four years. The present report contains information from fifty-seven countries, and among the many subjects covered are gross domestic product, composition of private consumption expenditure, government and revenue expenditure, and external transactions. It updates *A Survey of National Sources of Income Distribution Statistics.*

176. United Nations. Economic and Social Commission for Western Asia (ESCWA). *National Account Studies, Bulletin #8: Gross Domestic Product, National Disposable Income in the ESCWA Countries.* Baghdad, Iraq, 1986. 272 p. OCLC 13808818.
In 1973, it was established as Economic Commission for Western Asia (ECWA), and the name was changed to the above in 1985. This bulletin includes available data on national accounts during the period 1977 through 1984 for each country of the region as well as includes preliminary estimates for gross domestic product according to economic activities and expenditures at current prices for the year 1985. The publication is in English and Arabic.

177. United Nations. Industrial Development Organization (UNIDO). *Input-Output Tables for Developing Countries.* New York, 1985. 2 vols. OCLC 13271361.

Volume one contains twenty country tables, some of which contain detailed technical descriptions. Volume two contains sixteen tables for fifteen developing countries. The reference years of the tables range from 1970 to 1975. The tables in this volume provide a useful database for studies on the structure of developing economies.

178. United Nations. Statistical Office. *National Accounts Statistics: Main Aggregates and Detailed Tables, 1984.* New York, 1986. 1,784 p.

This is the twenty-eighth issue in this series showing detailed national accounts estimates for 160 countries and areas. The present publication forms part of a *National Account Statistics Series.* Other publications in the same series, issued separately, are *National Account Statistics: Analysis of Main Aggregates,* presenting in the form of analytical tables a summary of main national accounts aggregates extracted from this publication and supplemented by estimates made by the U.N. Statistical Office where official data are not available; and *National Account Statistics: Government Accounts and Tables,* showing some of the more detailed tables for the general government sector presented in this publication.

NATURAL RESOURCES

179. Dorner, Peter, and El-Shafie, Mahmoud A., ed. *Resources and Development: Natural Resource Policies and Economic Development in an Interdependent World.* Madison, WI: The University of Wisconsin Press, 1980. 500 p.

This volume is an integration and condensation of the proceedings of the Wisconsin Seminar on Natural Resource Policies in Relation to Economic Development and International Cooperation published in three volumes. Sponsored by the University's Institute of Environmental Studies and cosponsored by the Organization of Arab Petroleum Exporting Countries, the Arab Fund for Economic and Social Development, and the Kuwait Fund for Arab Economic Development, the seminar met in formal sessions at Madison three times a week during the 1977–78 academic year including a session in Kuwait. This publication, which summarizes the seminar presentations and discussions, provides a multidisclipinary perspective on the national and international role in regard to natural resources and its relationship to economic development and international cooperation. The materials in the book are grouped under four general headings. The first group, Natural Resources, focuses on the physical and economic dimensions of natural resources. The second group, Economic Development, is the major theme around which this volume is organized. Intrenational Cooperation is the third group, and it discusses the concept of intredependence among nations. The fourth group, Analytical and Policy Redirections, is devoted to discussing policymaking in the areas of resources and development at the national, regional, and international level. The chapters are logically related and provide a balanced and objective presentation of the subject.

180. Gabor, Dennis, and Colombo, U. *Beyond the Age of Waste: A Report to the Club of Rome.* 2d ed. New York: Pergamon Press, 1981. 239 p.

In 1973, the executive committee of the Club of Rome asked a group of club members, whose activities lay in scientific and technical fields, to assess whether the natural resources of the earth in terms of energy, materials, and food would be sufficient to sustain a growing population and allow its basic needs to be satistfied in the coming centuries. Consequently, a working party including a number of specialists outside of club membership was established to carry out the task, and this reports the results of its study under the direction of Nobel Prize winning physicist Dennis Gabor. The concept of waste management as epitomized in this book points the way for a better world. The text identifies the interconnectedness between food, agriculture, materials, energy, and human motivation. The underlying thesis of the book is that not only does wasteful operation of the economy present a threat to future generations, but the actual waste of human resources, through unemployment, underemployment, disease, malnutrition, and uncreative repetitive work which provides no satisfaction, is tragic in the present context and could deteriorate still further with the great wave of new population which is pending. This is a translation of the original work entitled *Oltre l'Eta dello Spreco.*

181. Mabro, Robert. *OPEC and the World Oil Market: The Genesis of the 1986 Price Crisis.* New York: Published by the Oxford University Press for the Oxford Institute for Energy Studies, 1986. OCLC 14243600.

The history of OPEC's attempts to regulate prices in the world petroleum market has involved notable successes and several crises. An analysis of the nature of these crises and of the causes and circumstances of their occurrence is crucial to the understanding of oil price movements and of the complex relationships between the actions and policies of OPEC and the behavior of the oil market. The book sheds important light on these issues. It also deals with issues of oil supply policies.

182. Organization of the Petroleum Exporting Countries (OPEC). *Annual Statistical Bulletin.* Vienna, Austria, 1965–. (Annual)

OPEC was established in 1960, "to unify and coordinate members' petroleum policies and to safeguard their interests," and in particular to maintain petroleum prices.

Published annually, data are provided on a variety of subjects related to oil. Among them are oil wells; production of natural gas and crude oil; refining; consumption of refined products; exports of crude oil, and refined products by OPEC member countries; world trade of natural gas, crude oil, and refined products; major pipelines in OPEC member countries; prices; oil revenues; and the financial situation of the major oil companies. The bulletin also contains data on population, area, national accounts, value of trade, and exchange rates for OPEC member countries. The 1985 issue, latest available, is the twenty-first in this series and contains 147 pages.

183. United Nations. Economic and Social Commission for Western Asia (ESCWA). *Arab Energy: Prospects to 2000.* New York: McGraw-Hill 1982. 212 p. OCLC 8505120.

The western Asia region possesses almost half of the world's oil reserves and meets about half the world's crude oil import needs. This study is a projection of energy supply and demand for the period up to the year 2000. This also gives an overall global energy picture including petroleum reserves, oil movements, past economic performance, and growth prospects.

184. United Nations. Economic Commission for Europe (ECE). *Long Term Perspective for Water Use and Supply in the ECE Region: Report on Recent Experience and Prospects for Time Horizons 1990 and 2000.* New York, 1981. 33+ p. OCLC 8555417.

This report has been prepared under the auspices of the ECE Committee on Water Problems. This is a long-term perspectives survey compiled for all countries within the area of competence of the ECE. These countries are situated in North America, Europe, and the Asian part of the U.S.S.R. It analyzes information and statistical data reflecting the past and the present situation and, in particular, future trends of water use and supply in individual ECE countries including the U.S. and Canada. It also outlines general trends for the development of advanced water use-oriented policies leading to a significant reduction of water wastage and more effective protection of water resources against pollution.

185. United Nations. Economic Commission for Europe (ECE). *Systems of Water Statistics in the ECE Region: A Report Prepared under the Auspices of the ECE Committee on Water Problems.* New York, 1986. 92+ p. OCLC 15365828.

The ECE Committee on Water Problems undertook surveys of statistics on water quality and use. These surveys, carried out over three years, entailed a review of the present situation and the outlook regarding relevant national systems of water statistics. The surveys drew upon information provided by the ECE governments including the U.S. Comparable systems of water-quality statsitics are essential in assessing the need for policies designed to prevent or reverse deterioration of the aquatic environment. Water authorities are not the only users of these statistics. Data are also of great importance for industry, agriculture, and the public at large. Well-founded water statistical data series thus have far-reaching applications.

POPULATION AND VITAL STATISTICS

186. Alderson, Michael Rowland. *International Mortality Statistics.* New York: Facts on File, 1981. 524 p. OCLC 6762014.

This book gives serial mortality of the twentieth century for European and other selected countries in tabular form by sex, calendar period, cause of death, and country. Data have been included for all those countries in Europe for which they have been available in a continuous sequence throughout this century, or at least for a greater part of it. In addition, a number of other developed countries have been included: U.S., Canada, Australia, New Zealand, Chile, Japan, and Turkey. For the majority of these countries, the material was available from the beginning of the century. However, some countries did not publish national data by cause until later in the second or third decades of the century. The data are tabulated for 178 causes of death, which have been selected to provide continuity over the greatest period of time.

187. Bennett, Gordon D. *World Population Problems.* Champaign, IL: Park Press, 1984. 258 p. OCLC 10631341.
It focuses on the problems of the people of the world, in particular the world overpopulation. The book is intended as a text for undergraduate college students, but it is highly readable, easy to understand, and concise in its treatment of the subject.

188. Faaland, Just, ed. *Population and the World Economy in the 21st Century.* New York: St. Martin's Press, 1982. 264 p. OCLC 8667564.
The Nobel Symposium on "Population Growth and World Development: A Fifty Year Perspective" was held at Noresund, Norway, near Oslo, on September 7–11, 1981. Its purpose was to explore long-term perspectives of world demographic and economic growth with particular emphasis on international differentials in demographic and economic characteristics, on resources and food supplies, and on implications for emerging patterns of international cooperation and conflict. This volume presents an overview prepared by the editor, the six background papers prepared for the symposium, and a summary of the discussions.

189. Murdoch, William W. *The Poverty of Nations: The Political Economy of Hunger and Population.* Baltimore, MD: Johns Hopkins University Press, 1980. 382 p.
This addresses the problems of uncontrolled population growth, starvation, and rural poverty as intimately related concerns with common roots in the institutionalized social and economic inequality of third world societies. It interprets current research in demographics, the economics of development, and agricultural economics to identify and define the underlying political and economic mechanisms that simultaneously encourage population growth and constrain agricultural production in the third world. The book is both scholarly and popular reading. It is divided into three parts containing eleven chapters. Part one is captioned "Population." Part two is "Food Supply and Agriculture." Part three deals with development. The first five chapters analyze the food and population problem in a straightforward way. Chapters six through eleven provide a conceptual framework for placing the problems of population and hunger in perspective.

190. Rodgers, Gerry. *Poverty and Population: Approaches and Evidence.* Geneva, Switzerland: ILO, 1984. 213 p.
This monograph is the outcome of an ILO research project on population, labor, and poverty financed by the U.N. Fund for Population Activities. There are many dimensions of poverty and population growth. The latter may be the cause of the former, and it also may be the obstacle to the former's elimination. Population growth may as well be the result of poverty rather than the reverse being true. Poverty involves not only basic consumption needs but also broader issues such as security, status, and job access and relative deprivation and inequality. The interactions with de-

mographic change vary greatly from one aspect of poverty to another. Some demographic factors enter into poverty by definition—mortality, life cycle factors, and patterns of household size and structure. Many other relevant issues affect behavior and welfare at the household level; family size, mortality, and migration can all have an incidence on poverty, but poverty in turn generates distinct patterns of demographic behavior. The evidence on all of these issues is reviewed.

191. United Nations. Department of International Economic and Social Affairs. *Estimates and Projections of Urban, Rural, and City Population, 1950–2025: The 1982 Assessment.* New York, 1985. 148 p. OCLC 11828456.
This report presents estimates and projections of the size and growth of the urban and rural population for all countries of the world and of the world's thirty-five largest agglomerations. These estimates and projections are the most recent biennal updates of urban-rural and city populations that have been carried out by the U.N.

192. United Nations. Department of International Economic and Social Affairs. *Global Estimates and Projections of Population by Sex and Age: The 1984 Assessment.* New York, 1987. OCLC 15625387.
This report presents the estimated and projected sex and age distributions according to the medium, high, and low variants for the years 1950–2025 for countries and areas generally with a population of 300,000 and over in 1980. The data for smaller countries are included in regional population totals and are not given separately. This report supplements *World Population Prospects: Estimates and Projections as Assessed in 1984* which presents a summary of findings of the estimates and projections as well as selected demographic indicators for every country of the world.

193. United Nations. Department of International Economic and Social Affairs. *International Migration Policies and Programs: A World Survey.* New York, 1982. OCLC 9273816.
This volume eighty of the Population Studies series, is the first study by the Population Division to present a survey of international migration policies and programs in the various regions of the world. This work is divided into five parts. Part one is "Permanent Immigration/Emigration." The salient point made in this chapter is that the number of places throughout the world for permanent immigrants has basically stabilized and may well decline in the future. Part two is "Labor Migration—Developed Countries" and examines the situation in Europe. Part three, "Labor Migration—Developing Countries," is an overview of migration policies in Africa, Asia, Latin America, and the Middle East. Part four, "Illegal Immigration," gives a regional overview; and part five, "Refugees" (those who are becoming an increasingly important component of international migration flows) are competing with more traditional migrants for a limited number of places in the major countries of resettlement.

194. United Nations. Department of International Economic and Social Affairs. *Population and Vital Statistics Report* New York, 1949–. (Quarterly, Annual) OCLC 11354595.

This publication updates population and vital statistics for over 200 countries and areas of the world. Included for each country are (1) results of the latest population census; (2) the latest official estimate of population; (3) a midyear population estimate for a recent year; and (4) the latest birth, death, and infant mortality statistics. The 1984 supplement (latest available) contains (1) estimates of midyear population: 1974–83; (2) population by age, sex, and urban/rural residence (each census): 1965–83; (3) live birth rates specific for age of mother: 1974–82; (4) mortality statistics: 1974–82.

195. United Nations. Department of International Economic and Social Affairs. *Population Distribution, Migration, and Development.* New York, 1984. 505 p. OCLC 12806663.

It is subtitled "Proceedings of the Expert Group on Population Distribution, Migration, and Development, Hammamet, Tunisia, 21–25 March, 1983." On the title page it also reads, "International Conference on Population, 1984." One of the issues of high priority of this conference was the relationships between population and social economic development. The conference focused attention on population distribution and migration and the ways in which these factors affect socioeconomic development goals.

196. United Nations. Department of International Economic and Social Affairs. *The Prospects of World Urbanization, Revised as of 1984–85.* New York, 1987. 268 p.

This is Population Studies number 101, and it presents the results of the latest study on the trends in and prospects for urban and rural population growth in the world. It includes estimates and projections of the aggregate urban and rural populations for all countries of the world, of the individual urban agglomerates that had populations of two million or more in 1985. For urban and rural population, the estimates and projections cover a seventy-five-year span from 1950 to 2025, and for urban agglomerations, the coverage is a fifty-year span from 1950 to 2000. This is the most recent biennial update of data on urban/rural populations and urban agglomerations carried out by the United Nations Secretariat.

197. United Nations. Department of International Economic and Social Affairs. *World Population Prospects: Estimates and Projections as Assessed in 1984.* New York, 1986. 330 p. OCLC 14629968.

A major activity of the Population Division of the Department of International Economic and Social Affairs is to provide up-to-date and internationally comparable estimates and projections of population and other major demographic variables for all countries. Between the years 1951 and 1982, the U.N. completed nine rounds of its demographic estimates and projections. The present report is based on the results of the tenth round—that is, the 1984 assessment of demographic trends. It lists figures and tables and gives estimates on such topics as life expectancy, crude death and birth rates, urbanization, international migration, and distribution of total world population by region for the period from 1950 to 2025 and in intervals of five years.

198. United Nations. Department of International Economic and Social Affairs. *World Population Trends, Population and Development Interrelations and Population Policies: 1983 Monitoring Report.* New York, 1985. 2 vols. OCLC 12852377.

Volume one is entitled "Population Trends," and volume two is "Population and Development Interrelations and Population Policies." These provide a general survey of the world population situation and development and includes special topics dealing with the interrelations among population, resources, the environment, and development. This report covers the period since 1974.

199. United Nations. Educational Scientific and Cultural Organization (UNESCO). *Statistical Yearbook.* Paris, 1963–. (Annual) OCLC 1607331.

This annual publication is prepared from replies to questionnaires and from publications received from member states of UNESCO and their national statistical services. It contains detailed statistical tables for education, science and technology, culture and communication, e.g., on population, area, exchange rates, expenditures for research and experimental development, book production, and paper consumption. The 1986 yearbook has about 900 pages and is in English, French, and Spanish.

200. United Nations. Educational Scientific and Cultural Organization (UNESCO). *UNESCO Statistical Digest.* Paris, 1984–. (Annual) OCLC 12223082.

Although the bulk of the data is taken from the UNESCO *Statistical Yearbook,* it is useful for general data items mainly of a demographic or economic nature. Data including the size of the population, its rate of growth, the crude birth and death rates, the infant mortality rate, the magnitude of the rural population, the illiteracy rate, GNP, and GDP (Gross Domestic Product) are presented for each of the 161 member states.

201. United States. Bureau of the Census. *World Population.* Washington, DC: U.S. Government Printing Office, 1975–. (Biennial) OCLC 15207459.

It starts out with a section of data for the world and summarizes demographic information for 200 countries and territories of the world with aggregated data for the world's regions and subregions. Although the currentness and quality of data available varies from country to country, this represents a most comprehensive source for this type of information. The 1983 issue, the latest issue examined, is subtitled "Recent Demographic Estimates for the Countries and Regions of the World," and it has 586 pages.

202. Vu, My T. *World Population Projections, 1985: Short and Long Term Estimates by Age and Sex: With Related Demographic Statistics.* Baltimore, MD: Johns Hopkins University Press, 1985. 451 p. OCLC 12668115.

This set of population projections was prepared for the World Bank's *World Development Report, 1985,* and, in fact, it replaces the *World Development Report, 1984.* Population projections are prepared separately for each country, and the results are presented at five-year intervals for the period 1980 through 2025 and at twenty-five-year intervals thereafter. This publication consists primarily of tables.

203. World Bank. *Population Change and Economic Development.* New York: Published for the World Bank by the Oxford University Press, 1985. 193 p. OCLC 12133101.

This study is a reprint with adaptations from the World Bank's annual *World Development Report, 1984.* It examines population change in developing countries and its links with economic development. The study shows why continuing rapid population growth on an ever larger base is likely to mean a lower quality of life for millions of people. It concludes that, in some countries, development may not be possible at all unless slower population growth can be achieved soon, before higher real incomes would bring down fertility spontaneously. The study outlines public policies to reduce fertility that are humane and affordable and that complement other development efforts, placing special emphasis on education for women and increased family planning serivces. The successful experience of many countries in implementing population policy particularly in the past decade, shows how much can be accomplished and how quickly. It is enriched by "Population Data Supplement" which includes tables for population projections and status of the women. It also has numerous multicolor maps and graphics and a statistical appendix.

PUBLIC FINANCE

204. Balassa, Bela; Barsony, Andre; and Richards, Anne. *The Balance of Payments Effects of External Shocks and of Policy Responses to These Shocks: In Non-OPEC Developing Countries.* Paris: OECD, 1981. 99 p. OCLC 8175668.

It is a comparative analysis of economic policy measures adopted by the developing countries in response to external shocks after 1973 and of the economic effects of these measures. It provides a clear understanding of the adjustment process in some regions of the world.

205. Bird, Graham R. *World Finance and Adjustment: An Agenda for Reform.* New York: St. Martin's Press, 1985. 353 p. OCLC 11815806.

Although it is a policy-oriented book on international finance, its usefulness is not limited to that field. The many useful statistical tables (e.g., unemployment in major industrial countries, 1963–83; economic growth for the same period; inflation, world prices, etc. also for the same period) and the succinct description of the performance of the world economy in the last two decades are its other welcome features.

206. Cox, Edwin B. *Bank Performance Annual.* Boston: Warren, Gorham & Lamont, 1986–. (Annual) OCLC 13088902.

Although the primary purpose of this book is to provide information on ways to enhance financial and operational performance of banks, it has statistical information of value to the study of economic conditions. Part three of the book lists "Banking Industry and Economic Statistics." The information therein presents indicators of size and performance for the leaders in banking, insurance, and finance companies and historical measures of change in the economy. This continues *Bank Performance Annual*, the older editions of which are more comprehensive and cover different subject areas, but the statistical themes remain the same.

207. Das, Dilip K. *Migration of Financial Resources to Developing Countries.* New York: St. Martin's Press, 1986. 263 p.
Transnational financial flows have been a significant factor of the multifaceted world economy, and the mulitlateral financial institutions, such as the World Bank, African Development Bank, and Asian Development Bank, have contributed to the interdependence between countries and country groups. The book examines the resource flows to developing countries from the international capital markets and the multilateral financial institutions as the sources of external resources. Various statistical time-series form part of the presentation.

208. Dennis, Geoffrey E. J. *International Financial Flows: A Statistical Handbook.* Lexington, MA: Lexington Books, 1984. 365 p.
The book deals with available statistical series on international financial data. It is divided into five main sections. Each of the first four considers a particular type of financial data, e.g., section four deals with "External Debt Statistics" covering the World Bank and the OECD. The final section gives an overall conclusion.

209. Dupuy, Trevor Nevitt; Hayes, Grace P.; and Andrews, John A. C. *The Almanac of World Military Power.* 4th ed. San Rafael, CA: Presidio Press, 1980. 418 p. OCLC 6086301.
In one volume, it contains an impressive compilation of data on the armed forces and military potential of every significant nation of the world. It also portrays economic strengths of each country by providing national statistics on area, population, GNP, fuel production, power output, merchant fleet, civil air fleet other than troop and equipment, and other national security information.

210. International Monetary Fund (IMF). *Annual Report of the Executive Board for the Financial Year Ended April 30, 1986.* Washington, DC, 1986. 177 p. (Annual) OCLC 5705422.
The annual report reviews IMF's activities, policies, organization, and administration and surveys the world economy with special emphasis on balance of payments, problems, exchange rates, world trade, international liquidity, and developments in the international monetary system. Appendices contain the major decisions taken by the executive board during the year, international reserves, financial reports, the administrative budget, and classification of countries. There are about thirty tables and charts containing financial statistical information. It is usually published in September, is also available in French and Spanish, and contains about 200 pages.

211. International Monetary Fund (IMF). *Annual Report on Exchange Arrangements and Exchange Restrictions.* Washington, DC, 1979–. (Annual) OCLC 1753642.

This continues the report previously entitled *Annual Report on Exchange Restrictions* which continued for the years 1950 through 1978. This report reviews exchange arrangements and summarizes the main developments in exchange controls and restrictions. It also surveys the progress that has been made in relaxing restrictions. Each report contains country-by-country descriptions of exchange systems and related measures in operation in member countries and provides a chronological list of the significant changes that have taken place during the year under review. The report also includes in tabular form a summary of the principal features of the exchange and trade systems of member countries. It is usually published in August and is over 500 pages.

212. International Monetary Fund (IMF). *Balance of Payment Statistics.* Washington, DC, 1981–. (Annual) OCLC 8020910.

This publication consists of monthly issues and a two-part yearbook containing balance of payments statistics for about 136 countries. The monthly issues contain aggregate presentations covering annual data and monthly, quarterly, or semiannual data where available. Part one of this publication gives detailed balance of payments figures including statistics for goods, services, and income. Part two provides about seventy tables of data featuring area and world totals of balance of payments components and aggregates. Because a country may change its balance of payments methodology, keeping track of such data can be difficult. For the years 1947 through 1980 it was entitled *Balance of Payments Yearbook.* Part of the yearbook used to be published in loose-leaf form which would eventually be incorporated into the annual volume.

213. International Monetary Fund (IMF). *Government Finance Statistics Yearbook.* Washington, DC, 1977–. (Annual)

A standard reference source on governemnts of IMF member countries, it brings together detailed data on revenues, grants, expenditures, lending and financing, and debt of central governments. The yearbook also provides information on the various units of government, government accounts, the enterprises and financial institutions that governments own and control, and the national sources of data on government operations. For state and local government finance within each country, there are parallel tables but in much less detail. Detailed statistical tables are presented on central government revenue and other related items. World tables are arranged by topic rather than by country, and this facilitates comparison between countries.

214. International Monetary Fund (IMF). *International Financial Statistics Yearbook.* Washington, DC, 1979–. (Annual) OCLC 5374371.

This is a standard source of international statistics on all aspects of domestic and international finance. It covers for most countries analyses of international payments, inflation and deflation, exchange rates, liquidity, money and banking, international trade, prices, production, government finance, and interest rates. Statistics are both historical and current, and cover annual statistics for thirty years. Also issued in French and Spanish.

215. Organization for Economic Cooperation and Development (OECD). *Balances of Payments of OECD Countries: 1965-1984.* Paris, 1986. 165 p. OCLC 14917597.
This publication brings together the main series of individual OECD countries', U.S. included, balances of payments for the period 1965 to 1984 and gives totals for the OECD area. Details on current invisible transactions (e.g., transfer payments) and capital movements are also presented. In addition, the principal analytical concepts are explained and national sources are indicated. This is bilingual: English and French.

216. Organization for Economic Cooperation and Development (OECD). *Bank Profitability; Financial Statements of Banks with Methodological Country Notes: 1980-1984.* Paris, 1987. 235 p. OCLC 15541043.
This gives the trends in bank profitability and factors affecting it. Such trends are major indicators of changes in the state of health of national banking systems. These OECD statistics on financial statements of banks provide a unique tool for analyzing developments in bank profitability during the period 1980 to 1984.

217. Organization for Economic Cooperation and Development (OECD). *OECD Financial Statistics.* Paris, 1969–. OCLC 7699565.
Beginning in 1980, it has been published in three separate parts. Part one, *Financial Statistical Monthly,* is in two parts and covers international and foreign bond issues and international bank loans, as well as domestic financial markets; part two, *Financial Accounts of OECD Countries,* an annual, has flow-of-funds and balance sheet accounting for twenty countries broken down by sector and financial instruments; and part three, *Non Financial Enterprises Financial Statements* (Annual), has balance sheets, statements of accounts, and uses of funds of a representative sample of private nonfinancial companies in half of the OECD countries. This is a bilingual publication in English and French.

218. Organization for Economic Cooperation and Development (OECD). *Personal Income Tax Systems under Changing Economic Conditions.* Paris, 1986. 381 p. OCLC 14100213.
Tax reform has become a major issue of public debate in many OECD countries including the U.S. in recent years because of widespread concern about high unemployment, slow economic growth, and low investment. This report analyzes developments in personal income tax systems in OECD member countries over the past decade and examines the policy choices facing the governments.

219. Organization for Economic Cooperation and Development (OECD). *Revenue Statistics of OECD Member Countries: 1965-1985.* Paris, 1985. 257 p. (Annual) OCLC 12675146.
The purpose of this annual bulletin is to provide internationally comparative data on tax levels and structures in OECD member countries with the exception of Iceland. The taxes of each country, including social security contributions, are presented in a standard framework. A special section compares the tax benefit position of a typical worker in each country. This is a bilingual publication in English and French.

220. Sivard, Ruth Leger. *World Military and Social Expenditures, 1982.* Leesburg, VA: World Priorities, 1982. 44 p. OCLC 2469505.
This provides an annual accounting of the use of world resources for social and military purposes. By pointing out that the burden of military expenditure is growing larger relative to the global economy, it is providing an objective basis for assessing relative priorities. It is highly readable and full of statistical and graphic information.

221. Snowden, P. N. *Emerging Risk in International Banking: Origins of Financial Vulnerability in the 1980s.* London: Allen and Unwin, 1985. 146 p.
The book discusses the safety of the international banking system, overindebtedness, economic and debt crises, and sustainable global economy and trade.

222. Tait, Alan A., and Heller, Peter S. *International Comparisons of Government Expenditure.* Washington, DC: IMF, 1982. 39 p. OCLC 8497615.
This publication provides a framework for comparisons of both functional and economic expenditure patterns of countries having similar economic and demographic positions. It also provides an implicit technological norm for predicting the economic characteristics of a country's expenditure pattern based on its choice of priorities for functional expenditures. Table 1 shows the international expenditure comparison index for comparing the functional categories of government expenditure.

223. World Bank. *Annual Report.* Washington, DC, 1946–. (Annual) OCLC 1443986.
It presents a summary and background of the activities of the World Bank Group during the fiscal year covered by the report. Chapters cover a brief review of bank operations, a global perpsective of the economic situation, bank policies, activities, and finances for the fiscal year and regional perspectives. It also reviews trends in lending by sector. The Statistical Annex to the report represents data on selected economic indicators, world trade, the flow of financial resources, external public debt, and international capital markets. The data are presented on a country and regional economic group basis.

TRADE

224. *International Marketing Data and Statistics.* London: Euromonitor Pulbications, 1975/76–. (Annual) OCLC 2636006.
This features marketing information on 130 countries in the Americas, Asia, Africa, and Oceania. It is an established source of statistical information covering the key economic, social, business, and market planning indicators for each of the countries.

225. International Monetary Fund (IMF). *Direction of Trade Statistics.* Washington, DC, 1958?–. (Monthly and annual).
This is issued by the IMF Statistics Bureau as a supplement to *International Financial Statistics.* Monthly issues present the latest available data on each country's total exports to, and total imports from, each other country with comparable data for the preceding year. A supplementary annual issue, usually in July, provides full-year data for a number of years with comparisons of the data of reporting and partner countries. First published in 1958, it replaced a similar publication called *Direction of International Trade,* which was jointly produced beginning in 1950 by the IMF, World Bank, and the U.N. Statistical Office.

226. Organization for Economic Cooperation and Development (OECD). *Foreign Trade by Commodities.* Paris, 1981–. (Annual) OCLC 10059444.
OECD bulletins of Foreign Trade Series C provides summary information of the value of trade flows of OECD member countries. The series are now published in one volume for imports and another for exports. The data cover all goods which add to or subtract from the resources of a country as a result of their movement into or out of the country. Values are expressed in dollars. This is a bilingual publication in English and French.

227. Organization for Economic Cooperation and Development (OECD). *Statistics of Foreign Trade.* Paris, 1959–. (Monthly, Annual) OCLC 1785576.
This publication is a three-part report. Series A is a "Monthly Bulletin" which gives summary trade figures for each of the OECD countries. Series B is "Trade by Country," an annual. Series C is "Commodities," also an annual. These series show total trade statistics for each country by partner country as well as by totals for main regions. They also give indices of volume and average value by country together with a breakdown of foreign trade values.

228. United Nations Conference on Trade and Development (UNCTAD). *Handbook of International Trade and Development Statistics.* New York, 1971–. (Irregular with annual supplements) OCLC 15925975.
The 1986 supplement is the latest available, and it updates the 1983 handbook. According to the Foreword, "The *Handbook* is intended to provide a complete basic collection of statistical data relevant to the analysis of the problems of world trade and development." The publication includes value of world trade by regions and countries; volume, unit value, and terms of trade index numbers by regions and commodity; net worth of world trade; summary by selected regions of origin and destination and structure of imports and exports by selected commodity groups; import and export for individual countries; financial flows, aid and balance of payments of developing countries; and some basic indicators of development. Data are presented for individual countries and for four major economic areas: developed market economy countries; socialist countries of Europe; socialist countries of Asia; and developing countries. The text is in English and French.

229. United Nations Conference on Trade and Development (UNCTAD). *Trade and Development Report, 1986.* New York, 1986. 172 p. OCLC 7973397.

This is the sixth in a series of annual reports begun in 1981. It provides both an integrated review of world development and an assessment of their impact on the trade and development of the developing countries. The present publication is divided into six chapters as follows: (1) The Depression of the 1980s and the Setback to Economic and Social Development; (2) The Macroeconomic Setting: Interaction of Policies in the Major Developed Market Economies; (3) The Tranmission of Growth and the Stability of the World Economy; (4) Deflation, Debt, and Trade; (5) The World Economy in 1985 and the Prospects for the Near Future; and (6) Debt, Growth, and Development: Prospects for the Future.

230. United Nations Conference on Trade and Development (UNCTAD). *Trends in World Production and Trade: Study by the UNCTAD Secretariat.* New York, 1983. 36 p. OCLC 10458685.

This examines on a global basis the principal trends in production and trade and identifies the major changes for a period of over twenty years. It is factual, analytical, and comprehensive despite its size.

231. United Nations Conference on Trade and Development (UNCTAD). *Trends, Policies, and Prospects in Trade among Countries Having Different Economic and Social Systems: Selected Studies.* New York, 1984. 145 p. OCLC 12005063.

This provides an apparaisal of the main developments in the economies and external economic relations of selected socialist countries of eastern Europe and selected developing countries. Information is provided on the evolution of trade flows, the institutional framework, and ways and means of promoting trade and economic cooperation in the context of trade relations among countries having different economic and social systems. Particular attention is given to the present situation and prospects for the development of trade and economic cooperation.

232. United Nations. Department of International Economic and Social Affairs. *International Trade Statistics Yearbook.* New York, 1985–. (Annual) OCLC 12857462.

This series began in 1950 under the title *Yearbook of International Trade Statistics.* With the 1983 volume, it changed its title to the present one. This yearbook provides the basic information for individual country's external trade peformances in terms of overall trends and current value as well as in volume and price, the importance of trading partners, and the significance of individual commodities imported and exported. Volume one contains detailed data for individual countries. Volume two contains, among other topics, chapters on price indices and commodity tables showing the total economic world trade of certain commodities. This set simplifies the comparison of exports and imports by country and by product. It also provides a most complete summary of international trade statistics. This is in English and French.

233. United Nations. Economic Commission for Africa (ECA). *Foreign Trade Statistics of Africa.* New York, 1966–. OCLC 294297.
The ECA was set up in 1958 to initiate and participate in measures for facilitating concerted action for the economic development of Africa and for maintaining and strengthening the economic relations of countries and territories of Africa, both among themselves and with other countries of the world. Its headquarters are in Addis Ababa.
Prior to 1966, it was published from Addis Ababa. The publication is in two series. Series A, "Direction of Trade," contains trade by country data in U.S. dollars for African countries for which data were available to the Secretariat of the ECA. The items shown are based on data furnished by individual reporting countries and territories in the form of the publications or tabulation listings. A companion of series A, series B provides cumulative yearly data on African commodity trade by region and by countries. Import and exports are analyzed by section, groups, and subgroups.

234. United Nations. Economic Commission for Europe (ECE). *Bulletin of Statistics on World Trade in Engineering Products, 1984.* New York, 1986. 407 p. OCLC 1486967.
The purpose of this bulletin is to show the flow of engineering products in world trade. Data given in this bulletin cover the export of thirty-six countries representing approximately 98 percent of total world trade in these commodities. Data is for the calendar year 1984 except for summary tables where earlier years are covered. The publication is purely statistical in character, and the text in the front pages and headings in tables are in English, French, and Russian.

235. United Nations. Food and Agriculture Organization (FAO). *FAO Trade Yearbook.* Rome, Italy, 1948?–. (Annual)
Began as *Yearbook of Food and Agriculture Statistics*, with volume twelve in 1958, it changed title to *Trade Yearbook* and continued through 1977 when the present title was introduced. Parallel titles have been used throughout in French and Spanish. The 1985 issue, the latest available, is the thirty-ninth in this series. Statistics in it are generally supplied by governments, and heavy use has been made of the data available from Eurostat, and official trade data have sometimes been supplemented by unofficial sources. The publication contains annual trade data for food and agricultural commodities and commodity groups. In most cases, quantity and value of exports and imports are shown for the three most recent years. The value of trade for several agricultural requisites, as well as the value of exports and imports by broader categories of commodity groupings arranged by country, are also shown. It contains index numbers of trade tabulated by major commodity groups and by economic classes and regions.

236. United Nations. General Agreement on Tariffs and Trade (GATT). *International Trade.* Geneva, Switzerland, 1953–. (Annual) OCLC 15113402.
GATT is a U.N. body concerned with rules for fair international trade. Set up in 1948 with headquarters in Geneva, it sets out common rules and obligations concerning international trading arrangements and a framework for the negotiation of agreements to liberalize world trade by removing

barriers and problems that fetter such trade. It is accepted by over ninety fully participating countries and over thirty participating under special arrangements, accounting altogether for over 80 percent of world trade.

This is an annual narrative account of world trade and includes useful data on recent trade patterns and developments. The arrangement of this publication is as follows: an introduction and general overview, a detailed consideration of commodity trading, a consideration of developed and developing countries and the eastern trading area, and finally a discussion of trade by geographic region. Unlike such compendia as the *Yearbook of International Trade Statistics*, this is primarily a narrative and analytical work. Thus, in effect, it acts as a companion to the yearbook.

237. United Nations. Industrial Development Organization (UNIDO). *Changing Patterns of Trade in World Industry: An Empirical Study of Revealed Comparative Advantage.* New York, 1982. 203 p. OCLC 9146252.

Between 1950 and 1970, the rate of world industrial growth exceeded that of any comparable period in the last century. This phenomenon, however, is largely confined to the developed countries. The statistical analysis in this book of 130 industries in over forty countries shows the changes in revealed comparative advantage that took place during the 1970s.

238. *World Trade Annual.* New York: Walker & Co, 1964–. (Annual) OCLC 1213196.

This series is published by agreement with the U.N. statistical office. It presents, in five volumes, details of the flow of trade of more than 1,300 items of the Standard Industrial Trade Classification (SITC) reported by each of twenty-four principal countries covering over 80 percent of world trade. Data in it are in commodity order for users interested in individual commodities. In the five volumes of the supplement, data are presented in geographical order of more than 154 partner countries that trade with the twenty-four reporting countries.

TRANSPORTATION

239. International Civil Aviation Organization (ICAO). *Civil Aviation Statistics of the World.* Montreal, PQ, 1975–. 174 p. (Annual)

The purpose and function of ICAO is to encourage orderly aviation growth and improve standards for aircraft navigation, airworthiness, and pilot licensing. This publication contains primarily summaries and selections of statistics reported to ICAO regularly by its contracting states on Air Transport Reporting Forms. The purpose is to present in one volume the most widely used statistical information on various aspects of civil aviation. Comprehensive and detailed statistical information on civil aviation in the world is published by ICAO in its various series of the *Digests of Statistics*. In addition, it issues circulars providing specific information of interest to contracting states. They include regional studies on the development of international air passenger, freight, and mail traffic and specialized studies of a worldwide nature. The above annual is also published separately in French, Spanish, and Russian.

240. *Shipping Statistics Yearbook, 1986.* London: Institute of Shipping Economics and Logistics; Bremen and Lloyds' Shipping Economics, 1986. 482 p.

This is a comprehensive statistical reference book for the world's maritime industries. Presented in it are statistical information for countries, country groups, and the world covering the world shipping market; its supply, demand, and trend; shipbuilding industry; its returns and trends; ports and sea canals; and world port traffic. Each part of the yearbook is preceded by a commentary written by Lloyds' Shipping Economist which summarizes and interprets recent market developments. Data are presented using percentage growth rates, indices, rank orderings, shares, and graphics as a way to facilitate interpretation.

241. United Nations Conference on Trade and Development (UNCTAD). *Review of Maritime Transport, 1985.* New York, 1986. 51+ p.

This is an annual publication prepared by the secretariat of UNCTAD. The purpose of this review is to outline and analyze the main developments in the world maritime transport in the past year and to assess expected future short-term developments. Emphasis is given to the developments of merchant marines in developing countries as compared with other groups.

242. United Nations. Economic Commission for Europe (ECE). *Statistics of Road Traffic Accidents in Europe.* New York, 1956–. 102 p. (Annual) OCLC 6039392.

This provides basic data on road traffic accidents and casualties in the European countries and the U.S. The scope of the statistics comprises road traffic accidents involving personal injury only. Data relate to accidents by nature of accidents and surrounding, accidents because of the influence of alcohol, and the number of persons killed or injured by category of road and age group. As far as possible, figures are given for the last two calendar years. This publication is purely statistical in character and is trilingual, in English, French, and Russian. The 1985 issue is the latest and thirty-second in this series.

243. *World Motor Vehicle Data.* Detroit, MI: Motor Vehicle Manufacturer's Association of the United States. 1944?–. (Annual) OCLC 1784678.

This is an informative resource document on production, imports, exports, registration, and sales of motor vehicles around the world. The continuing and growing internationalization of the industry is reflected in its coverage and presentation of data.

244. World Tourism Organization. *Tourism Compendium.* Madrid, Spain, 1983. 317 p.

This has been published every two years since 1975. The current edition includes two parts: part one contains historical series on world and regional trends of tourism supply and demand; part two contains statistical country profiles together with extensive data on domestic and international tourist movements, the use, occupancy, and capacity of accommodation facilities, and the economic and financial impact of tourism in each country.

WOMEN

245. International Labour Organization (ILO). *Women in Economic Activity: A Global Statistical Survey (1950–2000).* Geneva, Switzerland?, 1985. 170 p. OCLC 15681312.
This is a joint publication of the ILO and the U.N. Research and Training Institute for the Advancement of Women (INSTRAW). It is a global statistical survey of women's economic activity by geographical and economic region as well as by country. The statistical information contained in this survey presents ILO's labor force estimates and projections including national data on participation of women with regard to employment.

246. Joekes, Susan P. *Women in the World Economy: An INSTRAW Study.* New York: Oxford University Press, 1987. OCLC 1442900.
This study, under the auspices of INSTRAW, takes a long-term view of changes in the world economy to show their effect on the economic position of women in developing countries. Stressing the interlinkages between the macro and the micro levels of the economy, the book approaches the subject from two perspectives: the position of women who are engaged in gainful employment and the role of women in unpaid labor such as household work, farm work on their own land, and other activities that put them in the position of managing resources. Analyzing the employment trends for women by geographical region and by sector—including agriculture, industry, and services—the author assesses how the emergence of a modern, international economy has affected the economic position of women.

247. Organization for Economic Cooperation and Development (OECD). *The Integration of Women into the Economy.* Paris, 1985. 183 p. OCLC 12491037.
This report examines the position of women in the context of a range of economic, social, and institutional factors and identifies barriers to the full integration of women into the economy, focusing particularly on the period of rising concern since 1979.

248. Safilios-Rothschild, Constantina. *Socio-Economic Indicators of Women's Status in Developing Countries, 1970–1980.* New York: Population Council, 1986. 79 p; 220 p. OCLC 14910083.
The statistics on socioeconomic indicators of the status of third world women include men as well. The data cover forty-five indicators for seventy-five countries at the beginning and the end of the 1970–80 decade. The analysis of the data on different indicators is extensive.

249. United Nations. Department of International Economic and Social Affairs. *Economic Recession and Specific Population Groups.* New York, 1986. 99 p. OClC 14409785.
This deals with the effects of international stagnation and recession, especially during 1973–75 and 1981–83, on specific population groups, particu-

larly women. Although all types of countries are included, the focus is on developing countries. The analysis has particular bearing on how recession affects society as a whole.

250. United Nations. Department of International Economic and Social Affairs. *World Survey of the Role of Women in Development.* New York, 1986. 238 p. OCLC 14719945.
This survey, in pursuance of a U.N. General Assembly Resolution, consists of eight parts. Part one is an overview of the role of women in development in general. The other seven parts cover agriculture, industry, money and finance, science and technology, trade, energy, and the concept of self-reliance and the integration of women in development. It contains statistical tables.

251. United Nations. Economic Commission for Europe (ECE). *The Economic Role of Women in the ECE Region: Developments 1975/85.* New York, 1985. 94 p. OCLC 12741676.
This focuses on recent economic, social, and demographic developments which have influenced the economic situation of women in the ECE region. Various aspects of the role of women in the production of goods and services and the trends in their labor force participation, employment and unemployment, and pay differentials between men and women are covered. The analysis is essentially comparative, seeking both similarities and differences among varied groups of countries comprising the ECE region, the U.S. included.

252. United Nations. World Conference on Women, 1980. *Report of the World Conference of the United Nations Decade for Women: Equality, Development, and Peace: Copenhagen, 14 to 30 July 1980.* New York: United Nations, 1980. 238 p. OCLC 7061386.
The U.N. Decade for Women (1976–1985) stressed equality, development, and peace. The 1980 World Conference of the United Nations Decade for Women held in Copenhagen had similar aims and was particularly concerned with employment, health, and education of women in the third world. The focus of the report is a program of action at the national and international level, and the report is informative throughout on all aspects of the subject of the conference.

253. United States. Bureau of the Census. *Women of the World: 1984–1985.* Washington, DC, 1984–85. Various paging.
As part of an interagency project, a Women in Development database was established at the Bureau of the Census under the sponsorship of the Agency for International Development, containing statistics on a variety of demographic, social, and economic topics for 120 countries. The data were analyzed in detail in the following Women of the World Series publications: *Women of the World: Near East and North America,* by Mary Chamie; *Women of the World: Latin America and the Caribbean,* by Elsa Chaney; *Women of the World: Sub-Saharan Africa,* by Jeannie S. Newman; and *Women of the World: Asia and the Pacific,* by Nasra M. Shah. These handbooks present and analyze statistical data on women in these regions. They do not simply present information on women's status but also offer a critique on the concepts, availability, and quality of the data assembled. The handbooks are descriptive and exploratory in nature and strive toward

giving some explanation of the data and what the data mean. Overall, they provide the sociodemographic situation of women in these regions and explore female/male differentials over a range of variables which bear upon the status of women.

WORLD ECONOMY

254. Dornbusch, Rudiger. *Dollars, Debt, and Deficits.* Cambridge, MA: MIT Press, 1986. 240 p. OCLC 12837664.
This book brings together a collection of essays on economic policy problems of the world economy. The three topic areas, as mentioned in the title of the book, cover widely different policy problems. However, it makes sense to bring them together, beacuse international economic interdependence links exchange rates, budgets, adjustment opportunities, and debt service. The book is divided into three parts. In the first part, "Exchange Rate Theory and the Overvalued Dollar," the chapters cover the rise in the dollar, equilibrium and disequilibrium exchange rates, and flexible exchange rates and interdependence. Chapters in the second part, "The Debt Problems of Less Developed Countries," present three case studies in overborrowing and discuss the world debt problem from 1980 to 1984 and beyond. A concluding part, "Europe's Problems of Growth and Budget Deficits," takes up public debt, fiscal responsibility, sound currency, and full employment.

255. Fried, Edward R., and Owen, Henry D., ed. *The Future Role of the World Bank: Addresses by Robert S. McNamara . . . (et al.) Presented at a Conference at Brookings Institution on January 7, 1982.* Washington, DC: The Brookings Institution, 1982. 91 p. OCLC 8579406.
Since the inception of the World Bank at Breton Woods in 1944, it has been a major force in economic development and it has turned out to be the largest multilateral source of development financing in the world. It is also believed to be the most effective voice for economic efficiency and market-oriented policies in the developing world. Despite this record, U.S. support for the bank in recent years has been at its lowest ebb, and its future role is a matter of controversy. It is with this situation in mind that the Brookings Institution held the conference in 1982 to examine how the bank might adapt its role in this era of interdependence.

256. International Labor Organization (ILO). *World Recession and Global Interdependence: Effects on Employment, Poverty, and Policy Formation in Developing Countries.* Geneva, Switzerland, 1987. 139 p. OCLC 15353677.
This study describes the depression in the OECD countries with particular emphasis on the behavior of employment and real wages. It also describes how employment and real wages, in particular, behaved during the recession. Several important points emerge: the international financial and monetary system has failed to tepmer the decline in growth in the south, and the reliance of many developing countries on foreign capital has masked certain inappropriate structural features. The study also shows that

the declining growth in developing countries has had a reciprocal effect on the industrialized countries.

257. Lal, Deepak, and Wolf, Martin, ed. *Stagflation, Savings, and the State: Perspectives on the Global Economy.* New York: Oxford University Press, 1986. 402 p. OCLC 13062988.

This book contains the background papers prepared for the World Bank's *World Development Report 1984.* As the title suggests, the report seeks to put in historical and analytical perpsective the most recent recession in industrial countries, which unlike its predecessor was transmitted to developing countries. The report examines the causes of the "stagflation" that had plagued the industrial world in the 1970s, and its effects on developing countries, by asking whether the steady and sustained global growth of the 1950s and 1960s could be resumed. Although continuing to emphasize the importance of domestic policies in the developing countries, the 1984 report argued that the apparent problems of the global economy since the oil shock of 1973 are partly the result of a secular deterioration in the economic performance of industrial countries.

258. Organization for Economic Cooperation and Development (OECD). *OECD Economic Outlook.* Paris, 1967–. (2/yr.)

This is a journal of economic statistics and forecasts and provides a periodic assessment of economic trends and prospects in OECD countries. These developments largely determine the course of the world economy. Each issue contains an overall analysis of the latest economy trends and short-term forecasts. It appears twice a year in July and December and is both in English and in French. A separate publication, listed below, appearing once a year, presents historical statistics in analytical form.

259. Organization for Economic Cooperation and Development (OECD). *OECD Economic Outlook: Historical Statistics.* Paris, 1960–. (Annual) OCLC 9584471.

This annual publication accompanies the mid-year issue of the *OECD Economic Outlook.* It contains the same kind of data as are typically found in the more frequently published companion version, but it spans a period of twenty-five years. In general, data are not basic statistics but derived or analytical and are intended to display the movements of certain major economic variables, or alternatively, the structure or composition of certain economic aggregates. Almost all statistics shown in this publication are derived from the following regular OECD publications: *Labor Force Statistics* (Annual); *National Accounts* (Annual); *Main Economic Indicators* (Annual); *Statistics of Foreign Trade: Series A* (Monthly); *Statistics of Foreign Trade: Series C* (Annual); and *Indicators of Industrial Activity* (Quarterly). It is in English and French.

260. Organization for Economic Cooperation and Development (OECD). *OECD Economic Studies.* Paris, 1983–. (Semiannual) OCLC 10401210.

Title varies. This publication supercedes *OECD Economic Outlook Occasional Studies: 1970–1983.* This twice-yearly publication contains articles featuring applied macroeconomic and statistical analyses generally with an international or cross-country dimension. The 1986 autumn issue, for example, includes articles on tax, public debt, and developing country debt. The articles are scholarly.

261. Organization for Economic Cooperation and Development (OECD). *The OECD Observer.* Paris, 1962–. (Bimonthly)
The aim of this publication is to provide world economy information to the public. Coverage is given for most important OECD issues including facts and recommended solutions in such areas as economic growth, employment and unemployment, energy, multinational enterprises, finance markets, environment, science and technology, and aid to and trade with developing countries. Each issue emphasizes a specific topic. Regular features include highlights of OECD countries: Europe, North America, Japan, Australia, and New Zealand.

262. Starke, Linda, ed. *State of the World, 1985.* New York: W. W. Norton & Co., 1985. 301 p. OCLC 11798330.
This is a Worldwatch Institute Report on Progress Toward a Sustainable Society, and the book is subtitled as such. It is the second in this series. The first one, published in 1984, was highly acclaimed throughout the world as a global assessment of progress. It is an integrative document, cutting across discplines and fields of interest. It draws upon the findings of FAO's *State of the Food and Agriculture,* U.N. Fund for Population Activities' *State of the World's Population,* the IMF's *World Economic Outlook,* and other national and international surveys. The basic issues covered in the 1984 as well as the 1985 edition are food, population, energy, environment, and economic trends. The 1985 issue has devoted a section to population-induced climate change. The many statistical tables are highly informative.

263. United Nations. General Assembly. Fortieth Session. *Overall Socio-Economic Perspective of the World Economy to the Year 2000: Report by the Secretary General.* New York, 1985. 199 p. (Mimeographed)
This is a periodic assessment of long-term development trends and an updating of the world economic outlook through the remainder of the century. It is forward looking and presents a socioeconomic perspective to place recent trends in a longer term historical context in order to assess broad shifts in development patterns and progress. The analysis highlights the broader problems affecting the least developed countries, many of which are in the sub-Saharan part of Africa. It also reviews trends in military expenditures and various aspects of the relationship between disarmament and development.

264. United States. Bureau of Public Affairs. *Background Notes.* Washington, DC: U.S. Government Printing Office, 1964–. (Irregular) OCLC 7853031.
The caption title reads "Background Notes on Various Countries." This is a series of short, factual pamhplets about the various countries of the world. In four to eight pages, each note contains information about the people, history, geography, government, economy, political conditions, and foreign relations of the nation. The first page of each report is a profile containing brief statistical and factual information. The rest of the publication provides a broad overview of the country. The notes are revised on a

fairly regular basis, providing updates of several countries on a rotating basis throughout the year. Many of the materials give more information on large industrialized countries than on small developing nations.

265. United States. Central Intelligence Agency. *Handbook of Economic Statistics.* Washington, DC: U.S. Government Printing Office, 1975–. (Annual) OCLC 13957793.
It provides statistics for selected noncommunist countries and all the communist countries. The data for communist countries are official data from the country cited, CIA estimates, or estimates made by other organizations. It includes information on aggregative trends, foreign trade and aid, energy, minerals and metals, chemicals and rubber, manufacturing goods, forestry, agriculture, and transportation. Although it may vary somewhat from edition to edition, the usual basic economic statistics are there. Tables, charts, graphs, and maps are its common feature.

266. United States. Department of the Army. *Country Study Series.* Washington, DC: U.S. Government Printing Office, 1957?–.
This is prepared by a team of experts from the Foreign Area Studies Department of the American University under the Country Studies/Area Handbook Program. This is the DA Pamphlet 550 series. Each handbook in this series describes and analyzes the economic, military, political, and social systems of a foreign country, or grouping of foreign countries. Origins, traditions, and lifestyles are also featured. These handbooks are considered to be very good reference sources in providing a careful, detailed overview of a country. The studies are revised and updated irregularly. The titles published in, and prior to, 1977 are called *Area Handbooks*; revised and new titles after 1977 are designated *Country Studies*.

267. World Bank. *World Bank Country Studies.* Baltimore, MD: Johns Hopkins University Press, 1972–.
This series used to be called *Country Reports.* Some of the studies, in the present or previous series, have been published by the World Bank itself. These publications are general economic reports on individual countries that provide country information and in-depth analyses of the country's economic condition. These reports are often the only readily available and reliable source of comprehensive, up-to-date information on the economy of a developing country. About fifteen studies are published yearly, and the *World Bank Index of Publications*, an annual, lists the available reports.

Geographical Literature

AFRICA

268. *Africa Guide.* Saffron Walden, England: World of Information, 1977–. (Annual) OCLC 11540497.
Publisher varies. This guide used to be subtitled "Incorporating Economic Information from the Economist Intelligence Unit Ltd." This is a well-organized and informative reference work although studded with advertisements. The core of the work is country chapters. Statistical figures for each country on key economic, governmental, and tourist aspects are followed by a narrative part. The narrative part deals with the country's current position and emerging sociopolitical economic trends.

269. *Africa South of the Sahara.* London: Europa Publications, 1971–. (Annual) OCLC 1087495.
This provides an up-to-date survey of information about the political, social, and economic aspects of the continent and countries south of the Sahara. The book is divided into four parts: (1) Background to the Continent; (2) Regional Organizations; (3) Country Surveys; and (4) Other Reference Material. Part three, the major portion of the volume, contains a statistical survey for each country along with a narrative on the economy of the country.

270. *Africa Today.* London: Africa Books Ltd, 1981. 1,506 p. OCLC 9334568.
It is a comprehensive reference book on all the fifty-four countries that comprise the continent of Africa. It presents a detailed record of modern African history and the political, economic, and social development of each country examined from an African viewpoint. At the same time, it provides basic information on the activities of each country as an integral part of the continent as well as provides the role of Africa itself as part of the international community. In addition to the country profiles, the book also contains useful information about organizations concerned with Africa, e.g., the African Development Bank, the Economic Commission for Africa, the Economic Community of West African States, etc.

271. *The Cambridge Encyclopedia of Africa.* New York: Cambridge University Press, 1981. 492 p. OCLC 6249831.
This is a one-volume encyclopedia covering subjects such as the African past, contemporary Africa, government, utilization of natural resources, society, religion, art and recreation, physical environment, and interna-

tional relations and political economy. About one-fourth of the book is devoted to the discussion of African past. The "Comtemporary Africa" section provides sketchy profiles of fifty-four countries with short data tables for each country containing population and GNP information.

272. Ghosh, Pradip K., ed. *Developing Africa: A Modernization Perspective.* Westport, CT: Greenwood Press, 1984. OCLC 10324856.
This is the twentieth in a series of twenty publications entitled International Development Resource Books. Individual entries with annotations for all volumes considered relevant for this bibliography appear in the appropriate sections. The stated purpose of this series is to document and analyze current trends and provide the needed knowledge about the different sources of information and available data related to the topic of each volume. All the volumes are similar in format and organization and provide a comprehensive look at current issues, methods, strategies, policies, statistical information, comprehensive resource bibliography, and a directory of various information sources. Chapter one in these volumes contains a selection of reading materials on the subject of the particular book. Most of the information in the other chapters is repetitive.
   Part one of *Developing Africa* is a selection of prepublished articles on this topic. In this case, it is a reproduction of the World Bank publication, *Accelerated Development in Sub-Saharan Africa* (1981). Part two covers comparative economic data and social indicators in addition to statistical information about population, national accounts, etc., of thirty-three African countries. Part three provides an annotated bibliography of about 500 items grouped under eighteen different topics. Part four contains the directory of information sources.

273. Hodd, Michael. *African Economic Handbook.* London: Euromonitor Publications Limited, 1986. 335 p. OCLC 13794247.
The book considers the economic structure of the forty-seven African countries south of the Sahara, examines their economic performance over the past decade, and looks at their prospect for the next ten years. The first chapter considers Africa in comparison with other regions of the world. The second chapter compares the economic structure of the four regions. Each of the next four chapters is devoted to a region with profiles of three major countries in each region. About a third of the book is taken up by "Statistical Fact File" wherein basic data for the African countries are presented. This is arranged on a comparative basis so the country can be compared with the regional average and the eighteen countries classified by World Bank as industrial countries. Data are provided for population and land, economic structure and growth, education, and health indicators. Each of the large countries has a set of up to six graphs for 1973–83 charting real GDP, population, consumer prices, exchange rates, and merchandise export and import.

274. Mertz, Robert Anton, and Mertz, Pamela McDonald. *Arab Aid to Sub-Saharan Africa.* Munchen, Germany: Kaiser Grunewald; Distributed by Boulder, CO: Westview Press, 1983. 287 p. OCLC 11160184.
This report sets forth the results of analysis of the flows of bilateral and multilateral financial assisstance ($7 billion annually in the 70s) from Algeria, Iraq, Kuwait, Libya, Qatar, Saudi Arabia, and United Arab

Emirates to sub-Saharan Africa. The compilation of Arab aid statistics as presented in the forty-nine tables is perhaps the most extensive.

275. Organization for Economic Cooperation and Development (OECD). *Development Cooperation: 1986 Review.* Paris, 1987. 292 p.
This is an annual report issued since 1976. Part one consists of an overview and Africa's long-term prospects. Regular features of the review are chapters on recent trends in resource flows. There are special chapters on coordination, technical assisstance in support of improved economic management, agriculture, energy, and trends in aid to Africa. At the end, there is the much-valued statistical appendix.

276. Rose, Tore. *Crisis and Recovery in Sub-Saharan Africa.* Paris: OECD, 1985. 335 p. OCLC 13271062.
Sub-Saharan Africa's struggle for development in the 1970s has turned into a fight for survival in the 1980s which is what is portrayed in this publication. Part one gives Africa's critical economic malaise. Part two gives a review of the state of African agriculture. Part three addresses Africa's external trade, aid, and debt. Part four gives an overall view of the situation in the area.

277. United Nations. Economic and Social Commission for Western Asia (ESCWA). *Demographic and Related Socio-Economic Data Sheets for Countries of the Economic and Social Commission of Western Asia.* Baghdad, Iraq, 1985. 196+ p.
Established in 1973 as the Economic Commission for Western Asia (ECWA), it changed to its present name as listed above. This publication is the fourth in a series of data sheets covering population, labor force, and education. The benchmark date is 1984. It has twenty-three pages of exclusive Arabic text, and the publication is in English and French.

278. United Nations. Economic and Social Commission for Western Asia (ESCWA). *Statistical Abstract of the Region of the Economic and Social Commission for Western Asia, 1975–1984.* Baghdad, Iraq, 1986. 531 p.
Statistics for each country are presented in tables grouped into nine sections as follows: Population; Social Statistics; National Accounts; Agriculture, Forestry, and Fishing; Industry; Energy; Foreign Trade; Finance and Transport; and Communications and Tourism. The publication is in English and in Arabic.

279. United Nations. Economic and Social Commission for Western Asia (ESCWA). *Statistical Development in the External Sector of the ESCWA Region: Intraregional Trade and Trade with Other Developing Regions: 1975–1985.* Baghdad, Iraq, 1986. 511 p.
This publication is purely statistical in character, covering various aspects (commodity structure and direction) of the trade of the region. The series is detailed at the country, country-groupings, and regional levels and covers the period from 1975 to 1985.

280. United Nations. Economic Commission for Africa (ECA). *African Socio-Economic Indicators, 1983.* Addis Ababa, Ethiopia, 1986. 138 p.
The purpose of this issue (formerly, *African Economic Indicators*) is to convey the salient features of the socioeconomic trends in African countries for the years 1970 to 1982. It comprises three sections: (1) "Summary Review," which gives an assessment of socioeconomic development in the African region during 1970 through 1982; (2) "Tables and Charts," showing indicators for individual African countries; and (3) "Technical Notes," which provides brief description of the scope of the data presented. This is a bilingual publication, in English and French.

281. United Nations. Economic Commission for Africa (ECA). *African Statistical Yearbook.* Addis Ababa, Ethiopia, 1974–. (Annual) OCLC 2278564.
Title varies. This continues *Statistical Yearbook, 1970–1973.* The 1983 edition is the latest available. It is the seventh issue, and it is the combined edition for the years 1981, 1982, and 1983. As in the previous editions, the yearbook is published in four parts with the following subregional arrangements: part one, "North Africa"; part two, "West Africa"; part three, "Eastern and Southern Africa"; and part four, "Central Africa and Others in Africa." The 1983 edition presents data arranged on a country basis for fifty-two African countries for the years 1973 to 1982. Main topics presented are population, national accounts, agriculture, forestry, fishery, industry, and transport.

282. United Nations. Economic Commission for Africa (ECA). *ECA and Africa's Development, 1983–2008: A Preliminary Perspective Study.* Addis Ababa, Ethiopia, 1983. 103 p. OCLC 10336397.
The study is divided into four parts. Part one is an overview of Africa's present economic conditions. Part two analyzes the future of Africa by the year 2008 under the continuation of present socioeconomic trends and patterns at the national, regional, and international levels. Part three assesses the nature and content of the development scenario, and part four synthesizes the implications and choices for future Africa.

283. United Nations. Economic Commission for Africa (ECA). *Survey of Economic and Social Conditions in Africa, 1985–86.* Addis Ababa, Ethiopia, 1987. 175+ p. (Typescript in litho) OCLC 15100393.
Part one of this publication gives an overview of the region's economy and overall trends. Part two covers production of goods—agricultural, mineral, and manufacturing. Part three deals with human resources, transport, and communications. About a third of the publication deals with statistics consisting of thirty-six tables.

284. United Nations. Industrial Development Organization (UNIDO). *Africa in Figures, 1986.* Vienna, Austria 1986. 134 p. OCLC 15136280.
This has been prepared by the Industrial Statistics and Industrial Development Survey Section of UNIDO. This provides statistical indicators relevant to an international comparison of the process of industrialization in Africa. Figures are given generally from the period 1973 through 1983 with breakdowns as necessary and appropriate. The publication is in English and French.

ASIA

285. Asian Development Bank (ADB). *Key Indicators of Developing Member Countries of the ADB.* Manila, Philippines, 1970–. (Annual) OCLC 3507611.
It used to be published twice a year. Beginning with the July 1986 issue, it is now an annual. Also, with this issue, the People's Republic of China is included. The leading key indicators have been expanded to include the status of external debt.

286. *Far Eastern Economic Review.* Hong Kong: Far Eastern Economic Review Ltd., 1946–. (Weekly) OCLC 1568821.
Although a news magazine, it emphasizes economics, business, trade, and financial affairs. It covers all the countries of Asia, but the focus is on countries outside of South Asia. Each issue runs between seventy and 150 pages in length. In addition to articles which may run to about thirty pages, it has a number of regular features such as an economic monitor of a particular Asian country, company financial results, stock market results, and price trends.

287. Ghosh, Pradip K. *Developing South Asia: A Modernization Perspective.* Westport, CT: Greenwood Press 1984. 582 p. OCLC 10299786.
Like other volumes in the International Development Resource Books series, this publication documents and analyzes current trends. Part one is a selection of readings although some countries of the region are not covered. Part two provides statistical information from World Bank and ESCAP publications. Part three has an extensive bibliography of over 800 items. Part four contains a directory of information sources.

288. Khan, Azizur Rahman, and Lee, Eddy, ed. *Poverty in Rural Asia.* Bangkok, Thailand: Asian Employment Program, ILO, 1984. 276 p. OCLC 11680041.
This examines changes over time in the levels of poverty in the rural areas of Bangladesh, Pakistan, India, Nepal, Thailand, Indonesia, and Sri Lanka. It draws upon the most recent household income and expenditure survey (scattered over 100 statistical tables) and other data to analyze changes in rural poverty from the 1960s to the mid or late 1970s.

289. Krause, Lawrence B. and Sekiguchi, Sueo, ed. *Economic Interaction in the Pacific Basin.* Washington, DC: Brookings Institution, 1980. 269 p.
In an effort to understand how the economic impulses that originate in one country or in world markets are transmitted, the Brookings Institution and the Japan Economic Research Center sponsored a research project on the economic experience and policy reactions of six countries in the Pacific Basin in the 1970s. The countries selected for study represented a full spectrum of advanced and developing countries, rich and poor in national resources. An economist from each country analyzed his country's performance during a series of international economic upheavals—the breakdown of the Bretton Woods monetary system, the boom in raw material commodity prices, the oil crisis, and the subsequent worldwide recession

and weak recovery. This volume includes assessments of the economies of these six countries: Australia, Republic of Korea, the Philippines, Thailand, United States, and Japan. The results of the six studies are analyzed to determine how best to deal with internationally transmitted instability. In the concluding chapter, it is proposed that a regional organization begin to consider the common economic problems and opportunities of the Pacific Basin.

290. United Nations. Economic and Social Commission for Asia and the Pacific (ESCAP). *ASEAN and Pacific Economic Co-operation.* Bangkok, Thailand 1983. 365 p. OCLC 15627813.

Formed in 1967, the Association of South East Asian Nations (ASEAN) is the major body organizing cooperation in Southeast Asia and plays a leading role in facilitating economic, social, and cultural development and in promoting active coordination and mutual assisstance in matters of common interest and ensuring regional peace and stability. Although somewhat unrepresentative of the region as a whole, its membership includes Indonesia, Malaysia, the Philippines, Singapore, and Thailand.

This publication deals with cooperation ranging from trade, resource security, industrialization, investment, and technology transfer to monetary and institutional arrangements between ASEAN and some Pacific Basin countries. It provides an overview of the economic condition of the region, in general, and in agriculture, trade, and investment, in particular.

291. United Nations. Economic and Social Commission for Asia and the Pacific (ESCAP). *Economic and Social Survey of Asia and the Pacific.* Bangkok, Thailand 1974–. OCLC 2538563.

Prior to 1974, it was entitled *Economic Survey of Asia and the Far East.* As in previous years, the 1985 survey is presented in two parts. Part one contains a survey of recent economic and social development in the region in the context of the world economic situation. Part two is devoted to an analysis of international trade, trade policies, and development in the countries of the region. A brief appraisal of selected institutional arrangements for trade promotion in the region is also presented. The conclusions of these analyses have direct relevance to the policies of the countries of the region for the development of their domestic economies and the expansion of their international trade.

292. United Nations. Economic and Social Commission for Asia and the Pacific (ESCAP). *Electric Power in Asia and the Pacific.* New York, 1971–.

From 1951 to 1970, ESCAP issued an annual statistical publication on the subject. The issues covering the years 1951 through 1960 appeared in the form of a mimeographed "Electric Power Bulletin," and those for the years 1961 through 1970 appeared in printed form under the title *Electric Power in Asia and the Far East.* The current issue covers the years 1981 and 1982, and was published in 1984. Part one briefly reviews electric power development both in the region as a whole and in individual countries. Part two presents statistical data on technical and financial aspects of the industry in the respective countries. In this issue, information is also provided on hydro, geothermal, coal, oil, and gas.

293. United Nations. Economic and Social Commission for Asia and the Pacific (ESCAP). *Handbook on Agricultural Statistics for Asia and the Pacific, 1985.* Bangkok, Thailand?, 1986. 63 p. (In offset, stapled form)

This handbook contains statistical information on area harvested, production of selected agricultural crops, livestock and livestock produce, and production and consumption of fertilizers in countries of the region. It also contains tables on mid-year population estimates and agricultural population and data on land, irrigation, and other statistics related to agriculture. The scope of the data generally covers the years 1975 through 1985.

294. United Nations. Economic and Social Commission for Asia and the Pacific (ESCAP). *Launching of the Transport and Communications Decade for Asia and the Pacific: 1985-1994.* New York, 1985. OCLC 12897660.

This is, in fact, the special issue of *Transport and Communications Bulletin for Asia and the Pacific* (No. 57). The *Launching of the Transport and Communication Decade for Asia and the Pacific, 1985-94*, marks a milestone in the region's development, and it constituted recognition that the massive improvements required in transport and communications were a crucial element in the region's drive to realize the goals and aspirations of Asian and Pacific countries and more than half the world's population. The decade gave prominence to the fact that poverty and many other major economic and social problems confronting developing member countries were inseparably linked with the lack of adequate transport and communication facilities. This report contains an analysis of the nature of the problems and the means and methods to overcome them through cooperation and collective action.

295. United Nations Economic and Social Commission for Asia and the Pacific (ESCAP). *Statistical Indicators for Asia and the Pacific.* Bangkok, Thailand; New York, 1977?-. OCLC 4852898.

The indicators are issued quarterly in offset format, containing monthly and annual figures with related charts for the assessment of demographic and economic trends in countries of the region. It includes series on population, production, transport, internal and external trade, prices, finance, and national accounts. The March 1986 issue is the latest available and is volume sixteen.

296. United Nations. Industrial Development Organization (UNIDO). *Asian Industry in Figures; A Statistical Profile of Key Sectors in Selected ESCAP Countries.* Vienna, Austria?, 1983. 260 p. (Distribution limited) OCLC 10743193.

This document provides a detailed statistical analysis of the manufacturing sector, covering production and consumption of specific commodities as well as imports and exports in selected Asian countries. The countries covered are Afghanistan, Bangladesh, Burma, Hong Kong, India, Iran, Malaysia, Nepal, Pakistan, the Philippines, Republic of Korea, Singapore, Sri Lanka, and Thailand.

297. Wong, John. *ASEAN Economics in Perspective: A Comparative Study of Indonesia, Malaysia, Philippines, Singapore, and Thailand.* Philadelphia, PA: Institute for the Study of Human Issues, 1979. 217 p. OCLC 3892521.
This book is a crictical comparative analysis of the development status and prospects of five Southeast Asian economies—Indonesia, Malaysia, the Philippines, Singapore, and Thailand—which together constitute the Association of Southeast Asian Nations (ASEAN). The book deals comprehensively with topics such as the growth of regionalism, trade and development, intra- and extra-ASEAN economic relations, the process of industrialization, agricultural and rural development, socioeconomic issues of development, and the overall future outlook for the region.

CANADA

298. Canada. National Energy Board. *Canadian Energy: Supply and Demand, 1985–2005.* Ottawa, ON, 1986. 352 p. OCLC 15239843.
This report provides detailed informtaion on the assumptions, methodology, and results of the analysis of the supply and demand for energy in Canada. For each major form of energy, the report shows a supply and demand balance covering the period from 1985 to 2005. About two-thirds of the book is taken up by statistical tables.

299. Canada. Statistics Canada. *Canada Yearbook.* Ottawa, ON, 1905–. (Biennial)
Subtitle varies. The 1985 volume is subtitled "A Review of Economic, Social and Political Developments in Canada." Like its predecessors, it brings together a wealth of information to present a composite picture of Canada in a single volume and is considered to be the basic source of statistical data for Canada. Besides a chapter covering a "Review of the Economy," which has statistcal tables, it has other chapters with bearings on economy and related matters. One of the appendixes in the 1985 volume provides an economic chronology for the period June 1980 through May 1984.

300. Canada. Statistics Canada. *Human Activity and the Environment: A Statistical Compendium.* Ottawa, ON, 1986. 374 p. OCLC 15578590.
This provides a statistical overview of Canada's physical environment with particular reference to the interactions between human and other elements of the natural system. It focuses on the activities of the people in consuming resources, in building and reshaping landscapes, and in generating wastes, as well as on the impacts of these activities on the land, water, and air and on plants and animals. It is a source of pertinent statistics about the environment because it is also a guide to the wide variety of environment staistics available in Canada.

301. Canada. Statistics Canada. *Perspectives Canada III.* Ottawa, ON, 1980. 312 p. OCLC 6853858.
This is more than a collection of statistics. It provides a variety of perspectives on the economic and social features of Canadian life by means of descriptive essays which rely heavily on statistics. Social indica-

tors have been used synonymously with economic indicators in this book. It is divided into fifteen chapters including Population, Work Income and Consumption, Social Security, Leisure, and Vignettes of Canada and the United States. Most of the chapters are written by Statistics Canada officials and are highly readable.

302. *Canadian Almanac and Directory.* Toronto, ON: Copp, Clark, 1848–. (Annual) OCLC 1553032.
Title varies. Running since 1847, this is the oldest Canadian almanac. Data are generally organized under four major headings: Canadian Directory, Almanac Information, Canadian Information and Statistics, and Canadian Law Firms and Lawyers. An alphabetical table of contents precedes the body of the work and a detailed index follows. The statistics section tends to be the smallest and is sketchy.

CHINA

303. Barnett, A. Doak. *China's Economy in Global Perspective.* Washington, DC: Brookings Institution, 1981. 752 p. OCLC 7283541.
The rapid changes taking place in China's economy could have a strong influence on global problems especially in the fields of food and energy. This study analyzes the likely prospects for future growth in China's domestic economy and foreign trade and deals with China's role in the world food and energy systems and with future opportunities, problems, and policy issues in U.S.-China economic relations.

304. Chen, Edward, and Chin, Steve. *The Markets of Asia/Pacific—People's Republic of China.* New York: Facts on File, 1984. 124 p. OCLC 7464394.
Although it would appear to be a book of trade statistics, the bulk of it deals with economic statistics such as overall economic performance, household income and expenditure, and government expenditure and revenue. It has eighty-eight statistical tables presenting the Chinese economic, agricultural trade, and financial picture. This series of books under the title "The Markets of Asia/Pacific" is designed to provide an overview of the markets in one of the fastest growing areas of the world. The statistics in the above volume do give a useful analysis of China as a market, both consumer and industrial.

305. *China Yearbook.* Taipei, Taiwan: China Publishing Co., 1937–43–. OCLC 4184913.
This provides general information on the Republic of China, particularly its government, economy, transportation, educational system, social affairs, and foreign relations. In addition to the above sections, the 1980 edition (latest available) has a detailed section on "National Economy" and on "Transportation and Communications." Useful economic information may also be found under other sections, especially "Social Affairs."

306. Lim, Edwin. *China, Long-Term Development Issues and Options.* Baltimore, MD: Published for the World Bank by Johns Hopkins University Press, 1985. 183 p. OCLC 12666968.

This is a World Bank country economic report. World Bank country studies are reports originally prepared for internal use as part of the continuing analysis by the bank of the economic and related conditions of its developing member countries and of its dialogs with the governments of the reports. These reports are often published at a later date for public use. The World Bank untertook a study of some of the key development issues that China might face in their next twenty years and of some of the options for addressing these issues. This report summarizes the conlusions of that study. It is based primarily on the findings of an economic mission led by Edwin Lim and Adrian Wood who visited China in 1984. China's ambitious attempt to modernize and reform its economy will shape the future of not only the Chinese people, but also people throughout the world, and this report is expected to be a useful contribution in that regard.

307. Lippit, Victor D. *The Economic Development of China.* Armonk, NY: M. E. Sharp, Inc., 1987. 268 p. OCLC 14134773.

This book considers the economic development of China from the perspective of class interest and class structure. The book is divided into three parts. Part one lays out the analytical framework that underlies the study as a whole. Part two discusses the reasons for China's development failure prior to the middle of the twentieth century. Part three is devoted to the analysis of economic development in China since the founding of the People's Republic in 1949.

308. Organization for Economic Cooperation and Development (OECD). *Agriculture in China: Prospects for Production and Trade.* Paris, 1985. 84 p. OCLC 12600539.

This report analyzes major factors influencing food demand, agricultural production, and trade in China and includes a medium-term outlook to the end of the decade. It contains forty-seven tables of statistical information, primarily from China's State Bureau of Statistics, not generally available in Western sources.

309. People's Republic of China. State Statistical Bureau. *Almanac of China's Economy, 1981; With Economic Statistics for 1949–1980.* Hong Kong: Modern Cultural Co., 1982. 1,144 p. OCLC 9001422.

This is a significant reference book on China and its economic development. It is the first almanac of its kind to be published since the founding of the People's Republic of China and is "designed to provide a relatively complete picture of China's general economic situation including statistical data." Beginning with a detailed general survey of China, there follow fifty economic documents in the area of regulation and laws. There are over eighty articles covering agriculture, industry, finance, and transport and others that lead to a broad outline of Chinese economic research. Economic statistics are provided for the periods 1949 through 1979 and detailed figures are given for 1980. The section on the "Survey of China's Economy" gives a general review of the economic situation in the different sectors and regions of China during the past thirty-one years.

310. Townsend, James R., and Bush, Richard C., comps. *The People's Republic of China: A Basic Handbook.* 2d ed. New York: Published in cooperation with the China Council of the Asia Society. Distributor: Learning Resources in International Studies, 1981. 112 p. OCLC 7191763.

The book is divided into eight chapters as follows: Learning More about China; The Land and the People; History of the Chinese Revolution: China after Mao: Foreign Relations and National Defense; Economic Development; Foreign Trade and Material Welfare; Education, Public Health, and Daily Life. It is a concise and informative publication, but one must be aware of the statistics which are out of date.

311. World Bank. *China, Socialist Economic Development.* Washington, DC, 1983. 3 vols. OCLC 9756658.

The individual volumes are entitled as follows: volume one, The Economy, Statistical System, and Basic Data; volume two, The Economic Sectors, Agriculture, Industry, Energy, Transport, and External Trade and Finance; and volume three, The Social Sectors, Population, Health, Nutrition, and Education. Each volume has several statistical appendices, and they are volume one, Annex A. Statistical System, Annex B. Basic Statistical Tables; volume two, Annex C. Agricultural Development, Annex D. Challenges and Achievements in Industry, Annex E. Energy Sector, Annex F. Transport Sector, Annex G. External Trade and Finance; and volume three, Annex H. Population, Health, and Nutrition, and Annex I. Education. This is a World Bank country study based on the findings of an economic mission consisting of several teams which visited China in 1980. This is a definitive study on the economic conditions of China. It is factual, objective, and highly informative.

DEVELOPING COUNTRIES

[NOTE: "Developing Countries" is used in this section to mean third world, which is sometimes referred to as the "South." A list of the third world countries appears in the appendix. Three-quarters of the world's population lives here.]

312. Gauhar, Altaf, ed. *The Rich and the Poor: Development, Negotiations and Cooperation—An Assessment.* London: Third World Foundation for Social and Economic Studies, 1983. 273 p. OCLC 11206903.

The Third World Foundation and the Chinese Academy of Social Sciences invited seventy scholars and statesmen from the third world to the South-South Conference in Beijing (4–7 April, 1983), which came to be called South-South 1, to discuss the strategies of development, negotiations, and cooperation pursued by the developing countries during the last thirty years. The papers given at this conference are presented here and grouped as follows: part one, "Strategies of Development"; part two, "North-South Negotiations"; and part three, "South-South Cooperation." The appendix contains speeches by Premier Zhao Ziyang and other participants. According to the conference, among the major needs of the third world is a sustained intellectual effort to identify the impediments to cooperation with the North and to critically review its own record.

313. Ghosh, Pradip K., ed. *Development Policy and Planning: A Third World Perspective.* Westport, CT: Greenwood Press, 1984. 626 p. OCLC 10299431.

This is number eight in the twenty-volume International Development Resource Books series. Individual entries with annotations for all volumes considered relevant for this bibliography appear below. Several titles also appear elsewhere because of the overriding importance of their subject rather than the third world perspective. The stated purpose of this series is to document and analyze current trends and provide the needed knowledge about the different sources of information and available data related to the topic of each volume. Topics in these volumes generally relate to poverty, high rates of population growth, low rates of industrialization, dependence on agriculture, and high rates of unemployment. In all the volumes, the focus is on the availability of resources, human, natural, and capital, and in establishing policies and plans. The volumes were prepared under the auspices of the Center for International Development, University of Maryland, and the World Academy of Development and Cooperation. All the volumes are similar in format and organization and provide a comprehensive look at current issues, methods, strategies, policies, statistical information, and supplies a comprehensive resource bibliography and a directory of various information sources. Except for chapter one in these volumes, most of the information in the chapters is, by and large, repetitive.

Part one of this book is a reproduction of eighteen previously published volumes. Part two contains an annotated bibliography of data sources and statistical tables. Part three contains an annotated "Resource Bibliography" of 500 annotated books and a selected list of periodical articles and specialized publications. Part four is the directory of information sources.

314. Ghosh, Pradip K., ed. *Economic Integration and Third World Development.* Westport, CT: 1984. 397 p. OCLC 10348708.

This is number twelve in the International Development Resource Books series. Like other volumes in this series, this one is divided into four parts. Part one contains twelve previously published papers that present the issues relating to economic integration. Part two includes statistical information and a descriptive bibliography of data sources. Part three is an annotated bibliography of English language books, periodical articles and reports relating to the subject and published since 1970. Part four is a directory of information sources.

315. Ghosh, Pradip K., ed. *Economic Policy and Planning in Third World Development.* Westport, CT: Greenwood Press, 1984. 711 p. OCLC 10299438.

This is number seven in the International Development Resource Books series. It analyzes current trends in the development of an effective economic policy and planning of the third world countries and evaluates the progress made by them during the past decade in attaining long-term objectives of a sustained economic growth and improvement in the quality of living. Like other volumes in this series, it consists of four parts. Part two of the book includes statistical information, and there are over 100 statistical tables.

316. Ghosh, Pradip K., ed. *Energy Policy and Third World Development.* Westport, CT: Greenwood Press, 1984. 392 p. OCLC 10162648.
This is number four in the International Development Resource Books series. Like other volumes in this series, this one is divided into four parts. Part one consists of twelve selections of prepublished articles dealing with the global energy picture focusing in particular on the place of developing countries with respect to consumption, production, trade, and endowment in energy resources. Part two provides statistical information from the publication *Energy Supplies in Developing Countries* in addition to the usual World Bank sources. Part three is a bibliography, and part four is the directory of information sources.

317. Ghosh, Pradip K., ed. *Foreign Aid and Third World Development.* Westport, CT: Greenwood Press, 1984. 365 p. OCLC 10277700.
This is number ten in the International Development Resource Books series. Like others in this series, it is in four parts. Part one consists of eleven prepublished selections representing current international issues and trends affecting external assisstance in third world development. Part two contains the usual statistical information, part three, bibliography, and part four, directory of information sources.

318. Ghosh, Pradip K., ed. *Industrialization and Development, A Third World Perspective.* Westport, CT: Greenwood Press, 1984. 566 p. OCLC 10658268.
This is the first volume in the International Development Resource Books series. Like all the other published volumes in this series, it is divided into four parts. In part one, there are thirteen previously published articles which discuss the major issues in the industrial development of the third world. Part two is an extensive compendium of the principal international and comparative sources of statistical information and includes detailed tables and charts. Part three is an annotated bibliography of about 400 books, selected journal articles, and a listing of UNIDO publications. Part four is a directory of information sources.

319. Ghosh, Pradip K., ed. *International Trade and Third World Development.* Westport, CT: Greenwood Press, 1984. 569 p. OCLC 10402634.
This is number sixteen in the International Development Resource Books series. In keeping with the other volumes in this series, it has four parts. Part one contains nineteen previously published articles, mostly from the journal *Impact of Science on Society.* Part two contains statistical tables, part three, annotated bibliography, and part four, directory of information sources.

320. Ghosh, Pradip K., ed. *New International Economic Order: A Third World Perspective.* Westport, CT: Greenwood Press, 1984. 562 p. OCLC 10277743.
This is number nine in the International Development Resource Books series. As with other volumes in this series, it consists of four parts. Part

one includes twenty-two prepublished articles, many of which are from the journal *Impact of Science on Society*. Part two has the usual statistical information but taken from World Bank's *World Economic and Social Indicators and World Tables, 1980*. Part three contains the annotated bibliography, and part four, the directory of information sources.

321. Ghosh, Pradip K., ed. *Population, Environment, and Resources and Third World Development*. Westport, CT: Greenwood Press, 1984. 643 p. OCLC 10277675.
This is number five in the International Development Resource Books series. Part one, like other volumes in this series, provides a plan of reading materials on the subject. There are eighteen selections representing population, resource environment, and development in the third world. Part two contains statistical tables, and, in addition to the usual World Bank sources, it has the *Population Bulletin of the United Nations* as another source. Part three has about 400 annotated books, 400 selected periodical articles, and a list of some specialized publications. Part four is the directory of information sources.

322. Ghosh, Pradip K., ed. *Third World Development: A Basic Needs Approach*. Westport, CT: Greenwood Press, 1984. 435 p. OCLC 10458928.
This is number thirteen in the International Development Resource Books series. Like other volumes in this series, it has four parts. Part one has seventeen prepublished articles on the subject. Part two contains statistical tables preceded by a bibliography of data sources. Part three is the annotated bibliography, and part four is the directory of information sources.

323. Independent Commission on International Development Issues. *North-South: A Program for Survival*. Cambridge, MA: MIT, 1980. 304 p. OCLC 6025330.
Known as the Brandt Report, it is the result of an independent investigation by a group of international statesmen and leaders, headed by Willy Brandt, into the urgent problems of inequality and the failure of its economic system. The report takes its title from the belief that major international initiatives are needed if mankind is going to survive. For the hundreds of millions of people who live on the edge of starvation in developing coutnries, the South, this is a matter of obvious fact. The industrialized countries, the North, have not been willing in the past to go very far toward accepting the South's case that the world economy works to the disadvantage of the South. With striking unanimity, the eighteen members of the commission coming from five continents and representing industrialized as well as developing nations have agreed on a set of bold recommendations including a new approach to international finance and development of the monetary system. They propose long-term reforms by the year 2000, priority programs for the 1980s, and emergency action to avert an economic crisis. Official reactions of governments and institutions including the U.N. were such that there was a call to make the report obligatory reading for all citizens of the world. A companion volume, *Handbook of World Development: The Guide to the Brandt Report*, supplements this and helps in understanding the recommendations in it.

324. Killick, Tony, ed. *The IMF and Stabilization: Developing Country Experiences.* New York: St. Martin's Press, 1984. 216 p. OCLC 9970649.

This studies the policies of the IMF with particular reference to balance of payments management in Latin America, Indonesia, Jamaica, and Kenya. The authors consider the means available to developing countries to stabilize their economies and examine the effect of the conditionality of IMF's stabilization program. This is part of a two-volume study, the second volume being entitled *The Quest for Economic Stabilization: The IMF and the Third World.* The second volume deals with methodology and treats the subject in a general manner.

325. Lloyd, Peter Cutt. *A Third World Proletariat?* Boston: G. Allen & Unwin, 1982. 139 p. OCLC 7837227.

The book focuses upon countries most of which lie in the tropics, have an indigenous or non-Western cultural heritage, and have experienced colonial rule. The processes of economic development taking place in these countries replicate those of the industrial nations of the West, and the social structures of the former are converging toward those patterns visible in the latter. Two-thirds of the population of the cities in these countries are described as the urban poor.

326. Mathur, Kamal. *Economic Development in the Third World Countries: With Special Reference to Income Differentials in the ESCAP Region.* New Delhi, India: Associated Publishing House, 1983. 209 p.

This study concentrates on the measurement of income differentials and qualitative analysis of the sources of economic growth in six countries—two developed, two semideveloped, and two less developed—of the Asian and Pacific region. It examines the causes of different growth experiences and verifies that, despite planned utilization of resources and development potentials, there had been wide variations in the growth rates among countries of the ESCAP region. It has been observed that some countries have experienced virtual stagnation, whereas others have registered dramatic increases.

327. Organization for Economic Cooperation and Development (OECD). *Twenty-Five Years of Development Cooperation: A Review, 1985 Report.* Paris, 1985. 337 p.

The 1985 edition of the report marks the twenty-fifth anniversary of the Development Assistance Committee of the OECD. It covers not only the latest year but a quarter century of large-scale economic assistance, and in some respects its coverage is the entire forty-year period since World War II. It assesses the main successes and failures of the program and draws lessons for the future. The observations are brought to bear on the ways to make aid more effective.

328. Ray, S. K. *Economics of the Third World.* New Delhi, India: Prentice-Hall of India, 1983. 415 p. OCLC 9802901.

It is a treatise on the fundamental economic problems relating to growth and development in forty-seven developing countries with in-depth analyses of some vital economic phenomena in eighteen of them. In the concluding chapter, an incisive analysis of the world situation in the context of North-South development is made.

329. Reynolds, Lloyd George. *Economic Growth in the Third World, 1850-1980.* New Haven, CT: Yale University Press, 1985. 469 p. OCLC 11112544.
This is a publication of the Economic Growth Center of Yale University. It analyzes the process of economic growth and the economic relations between the developing and the developed nations. It is a factual account of the economic conditions of developing countries with considerable emphasis on the past.

330. Stephenson, Peter. *Handbook of World Development: The Guide to the Brandt Report.* New York: Holmes & Meier Publisher, Inc., 1981. 177 p.
This book is in two alphabetical sequences. The first one, termed subject entries, provides the facts and explanations on the main issues considered by the Independent Commission on International Development Issues published under the title *North-South: A Program For Survival* (also known as the Brandt Report). The second sequence, termed country entries, provides essential information about the 100 countries of the third world that constitute the Brandt Report's South. The subject entries consist of the themes and facts covered in the report and the actions that it urged. Most entries contain a quotation from the report, and it is usually followed by a page reference to it. Although the handbook is intended as a supplement to the report, and it helps in clearer understanding of the specific recommendations in it, it can by itself be used as a source of information.

331. Taylor, Philip, and Raymond, Gregory A., ed. *Third World Policies of Industrialized Nations.* Westport, CT: Greenwood Press, 1982. 282 p. OCLC 7876419.
The major concern of this book is the widening economic gap between the industrial nations and the third world. It is designed as an introduction to the foreign economic policies that the major industrialized nations have undertaken when interacting with the less developing countries of Africa, Asia, and Latin America. Part one of the book contains an analysis of the behavior of the European nations (the U.K., France, the Federal Republic of Germany, and Italy). Part two focuses on the U.S., Canada, and Japan. Part three examines The Netherlands, the European Community, and the Soviet Union. In the last chapter, some conclusions are drawn regarding the foreign economic policies of these states.

332. United Nations Conference on Trade and Development (UNCTAD). *The Least Developed Countries, 1985 Report.* New York, 1986. 437+ p.
There are thirty-six countries classified by the U.N. as the least developed among the developing nations. Most of these countries live in abject poverty, and the continuing economic deterioration of these countries has been of great concern to the international community. The present report contains an assessment of the socioeconomic development in the least developed coutnries since 1980. It is also a review of international support and of developments in the economies of these countries in the 80s. It contains a compendium of basic data relating to these countries.

333. United Nations. Department of International Economic and Social Affairs. *Living Conditions in Developing Countries in the Mid-1980s.* New York, 1986. 64 p.

This supplements and updates *1985 Report on the World Social Situation.* It brings together in summary form information on different aspects of living conditions in developing countries collected in different parts of the U.N. system. Emphasis is placed on the links among different elements of well-being, and major policy issues are analyzed. The chapters deal specifically with income, employment and poverty, mortality and life expectancy, health and socioeconomic environment, food and nutrition, shelter, and literacy.

334. United Nations. Department of International Economic and Social Affairs. *1985 Report on the World Social Situation.* New York, 1985. 101 p. OCLC 13827584.

This is the eleventh in a series of reports on this subject dating from 1952. This report provides a global overview retaining special attention to regional and other perspectives in social and overall development. It focuses on major obstacles to social progress as well as on the forces of worldwide social change, particularly education, technology, communications, urbanization, employment patterns, and the role of the state. It is divided into two parts. Part one is devoted to a discussion of major obstacles to social progress. It has three chapters as follows: chapter one, "Underdevelopment and the Difficulties of International Economic Cooperation"; chapter two, "Conflicts and Militarism"; and chapter three, "Violence to Groups and Individuals." Part two analyzes pervasive forces of social change. This publication is indeed a thought-provoking report, and it is well documented.

335. United States. Bureau of the Census. *Women at Work: A Chartbook.* Washington, DC: U.S. Government Printing Office, 1985. 70 p. OCLC 12086554.

This report presents a series of captioned charts describing the situation of women in selected developing countries based on coherent statistics including those analyzed in the reports in the *Women of the World* series. As part of an integrating project, a Women in Development database was established at the Bureau of the Census under the sponsorship of the U.S. Agency for International Development, containing statistics on a variety of demographic, social, and economic topics for 120 countries. The data for developing countries were analyzed in detail in these reports. This chartbook focuses on women's economic activity, labor force trends, occupational and industrial employment patterns, unemployment, and market work of women in the family context. It is organized by topic. Within each topic, charts are presented by region, and within each chart, data are shown by country. All of the topics presented are important the world over, but women's situations with respect to each of them differ widely among the world's regions or even among countries within the region.

EUROPE

336. *European Marketing Data and Statistics (EMDAS)*. London: European Research Consultants Ltd., 1962–. (Annual) OCLC 1969204.
It uses EMDAS as its other title. This is a comrehensive summary of the latest published statistics on all basic marketing parameters. The subjects covered include employment, production, standards of living, market sizes, retailing, consumer expenditure, housing, health, education, communications, tourism, culture, and mass media. The 1986 edition is the latest available and has over 350 statistical tables that furnish at-a-glance comparisons of various countries. It is established as a valued source of reference of market information on the thirty countries of western and eastern Europe. It incorporates statistical information published by the statistical offices within the various countries and by a wide range of European associations and organizations.

337. Organization for Economic Cooperation and Development (OECD). *OECD Economic Surveys*. Paris, 1953–. (Annual) OCLC 10157875.
This was originally part of the *OECD Annual Report* for the years 1949 through 1952, and later, it became *Economic Conditions in Member and Associated Countries*. From the mid-60s, it has been issued under the title as listed in the above citation. This is an annual survey of economic development and prospects in each OECD country. Separate annual reviews for each of the twenty-four OECD member countries are issued under this series. This provides a discussion of recent trends, economic policy, and prospects for the coming year. A "Statistical Annex" in each survey usually contains statistics for basic economic indicators, such as national accounts, production, employment and labor market, foreign trade, balance of payments, money supply, and counterparts, and all of these usually for a ten-year period. Because these booklets are revised annually, the information they contain is generally more current than that found in other publications. These surveys give more detail than is available in *Economic Outlook*.

338. United Nations. Economic Commission for Europe (ECE). *Annual Bulletin of Coal Statistics for Europe*. New York, 1966–. (Annual) OCLC 2906112.
The purpose of this bulletin is to provide basic data on developments and trends in the field of solid fuels in European countries, Canada, and the U.S. Beginning with the 1983 issue, world summary of solid fuel production is also given. This bulletin is supplemented by *Quarterly Bulletin of Coal Statistics for Europe*. Both publications are statistical in character and figures are given for the last four years. For an analysis of the coal situation and its prospects, reference may be made to the periodic reviews prepared by the ECE listed in the appendix of each bulletin. Title and text of this publication is in English, French, and Russian. The 1985 annual volume (published in 1986) is the twentieth issue, is the latest available, and has ninety-one pages.

339. United Nations. Economic Commission for Europe (ECE). *Annual Bulletin of Electric Energy Statistics for Europe.* New York, 1955–. (Annual) OCLC 1483422.

The purpose of this bulletin is to provide basic data on developments and trends in the field of electric energy in European countries, Canada, and the U.S. The data refer to capacity of plants; production; consumption; supplies to consumers; comsumption fuels; and corresponding production of electric energy, trade, and international exchanges. This publication is purely statistical in character, and figures are given for the last four years. Titles and text are in English, French, and Russian. The 1984 volume, published in 1985, is the thirtieth issue and has 101 pages.

340. United Nations. Economic Commission for Europe (ECE). *Annual Bulletin of Gas Statistics for Europe, 1985.* New York, 1986. 106 p. (Annual).

The 1985 volume is the thirty-first issue in this series. The purpose of this bulletin is to provide basic data on developments and trends in the field of gaseous fuels in Europe, Canada, and the U.S. The data refer to production, stocks, inland availability, deliveries, trade, substitute natural gas, etc. This publication is purely statistical in character, and figures are given for the last four years. Title and text are in English, French, and Russian.

341. United Nations. Economic Commission for Europe (ECE). *Annual Bulletin of General Energy Statistics for Europe.* New York, 1968–. (Annual) OCLC 1486704.

This provides data on the energy situation as a whole in European countries, Canada, and the U.S. The data, purely statistical in nature, relate to the last two years. The 1984 volume, published in 1986 is the latest available and has 122 pages. Title and text are in English, French, and Russian.

342. United Nations. Economic Commission for Europe (ECE). *Annual Bulletin of Housing and Building Statistics for Europe.* New York, 1957–. (Annual) OCLC 1261977.

This provides basic data on trends in the field of housing and building in European countries, Canada, and the U.S. Beginning with the 1982 edition, the scope has been expanded to include dwelling stock and structure of dwelling construction; dwellings completed by type of investors, by type of material used for low bearing structure, energy consumption by household, consumer price, and rent indices; value of construction; employment in the construction industry; and hosts of other information relating to the industry. Figures are given for the last four years. It is in English, French, and Russian. The 1985 volume (published in 1986) is the twenty-ninth issue and has 103 pages.

343. United Nations. Economic Commission for Europe (ECE). *Annual Bulletin of Transport Statistics for Europe 1985.* New York, 1987. 267 p. OCLC 1768055.

The 1985 volume is the thirty-seventh issue. The purpose of this bulletin is to provide basic data on trade and related trends in European countries, Canada, and the U.S. This publication is purely statistical in character. The scope of the statistics comprises the rail, road and inland waterways sectors, container transport goods loaded and unloaded at seaports, and transport by oil pipeline and internal goods transport by various modes of transport and commodity group. Title and text are in English, French, and Russian.

344. United Nations. Economic Commission for Europe (ECE). *Economic Survey of Europe.* Geneva, Switzerland, 1946–47–; New York, 1948–. (Annual) OCLC 14562943.
Title varies. The report is divided into five chapters and appendixes. Chapter one covers the economic situation in the ECE region including global developments. Chapter two deals with market economies of Europe and North America. Chapter three covers eastern Europe and the Soviet Union. Chapter four takes up Five Year Plans (1986–90) in eastern Europe and the Soviet Union. Chapter five deals with East-West economic relations. The appendix tables show annual changes in main economic indicators for the period 1970–86. The data are presented in three sections: section A provides macroeconomic indicators for the ECE market economies. Appendix B does the same for eastern Europe and the Soviet Union, and Appendix C covers world trade and the development of foregn trade of the ECE countries. The 1986–87 survey is the fortieth in this series and is the latest available, and as in previous editions, it is full of statistical tables, charts, and bar graphs.

Eastern Europe

345. Nenov, Zhivko Ivanov. *Trade and Cooperation between the Socialist Countries of Eastern Europe and Developing Countries in the Field of Food and Agriculture: Study.* New York, 1985. 23 p. OCLC 12981612.
Published under the auspices of the United Nations Conference on Trade and Development, it provides information about trade and cooperation between the socialist countries of eastern Europe and the developing countries in the field of food and agriculture. It also contains bibliographic references.

346. Vienna Institute for Comparative Economic Studies. *COMECON Data.* Westport, CT: Greenwood Press, 1981–. (Biennial) OCLC 7769689.
Eastern European nations have formed an organization of economic cooperation similar to the Common Market in western Europe. Their organization is called the Council for Mutual Economic Assistance (CMEA, also referred to as COMECON). Under COMECON, each nation is supposed to specialize in certain kinds of production. COMECON has not been entirely successful, partly because the Soviet Union has so much more economic power than the other member nations. It was originally founded in 1949 by the U.S.S.R., Bulgaria, Czecholslovakia, Hungary, Poland, and Romania. Later admissions were the German Democratic Republic, Mongolia, Cuba, Vietnam, and Yugoslavia. Afganistan, Angola, Ethiopia, Laos, Mexico, Mozambique, Nicaragua, and the People's Democratic Republic of Yemen are observers.
    This is published alternately with *COMECON Foreign Trade Data.* Title and publisher vary. The 1985 edition of this book is published by

Macmillan Press Ltd. of London and is the fourth in this series. It presents information on the economies of the European CMEA countries since 1960 and is arranged by broad subject groupings and then by individual countries. The data originate from three distinct groups of sources: (1) official statistical yearbooks and periodicals published by the member countries of COMECON and the statistical yearbook of the CMEA secretariat, supplemented by publications of Yugoslavia; (2) data published by international organizations, e.g., United Nations, ECE, OECD, IMF, the World Bank; and (3) Western sources. More than fifty titles—statistical yearbooks and periodicals from CMEA countries and of international organizations—are listed under sources.

347. Vienna Institute for Comparative Economic Studies. *COMECON Foreign Trade Data.* Westport, CT: Greenwood Press, 1981–. (Biennial) OCLC 7763464.
This is published alternately with *COMECON Data* and covers exports and imports by trading partners and for selected commodities for the seven constituent parts of COMECON as mentioned in the preceding publication. The statistics are presented as graphs and tables, growth rates, and percentages in most cases.

European Communities

348. European Communities. *The Agricultural Situation in the Community; 1985 Report.* Luxembourg, 1985. 439 p. OCLC 9799280.
This is the eleventh report on the agricultural situation in the community. It is in two parts. The first part covers the main events in 1985: the general economic and political context, developments on the agriculture market, the economic situation of the farmers and consumers, etc. The second part is a sizeable statistical annex providing in a single grouping all the main statistics needed for a proper understanding of the agricultural economy and various aspects of community agriculture.

349. European Communities. Eurostat. *Consumer Prices in the EC, 1980.* Luxembourg, 1983. 189 p. OCLC 10541352.
This is the result of a major survey of the prices of goods and services which forms part of the final consumption of households and took place in the ten capitals of the member countries and in Madrid and Lisbon. This survey was part of a volume comparison of the principal aggregates of the national accounts. It is in the major languages of the community.

350. European Communities. Eurostat. *Demographic Statistics.* Luxembourg, 1978–. (Annual)
This provides comparable and up-to-date information for individual member countries as well as the community as a whole. The principal series of demographic statistics including population by sex and age groups, births, deaths, migration, marriages, divorces, fertility, life expectancy, and population projections are given. The 1986 issue is the latest available; it has 220 pages and is in major languages of the community.

351. European Communities. Eurostat. *Industry Statistical Yearbook, 1985.* Luxembourg, 1986. Vol. 46. 147 p.

This gives an overview of industry in the European Community and illustrates its position as part of the European economy as a whole and as compared with the U.S. and Japan. It is a clear, concise, and easy-to-use survey of the community industry.

352. European Communities. Eurostat. *Labour Force Survey: Results 1984.* Luxembourg, 1986. 161 p.

This provides the detailed results of the 1984 community labor force survey. A long standing feature of this survey is its ability both to provide results which are more comparable between countries than those available from other sources and to highlight certain characteristics of the labor market for which information is lacking elsewhere. The 1984 survey is the second in the new series of surveys introduced in 1983 which the European Communities Commission intends to hold annually as long as labor market problems and changing employment structures warrant it.

353. European Communities. Eurostat. *Regions Statistical Yearbook.* Luxembourg, 1986. (Annual) OCLC 15135527.

It contains unemployment rates, main regional indicators, labor force data, etc., and gives explanatory notes and a map of the region. The text is in Danish, Dutch, English, French, German, Greek, and Italian.

354. European Communities. Eurostat. *Yearbook of Regional Statistics.* Luxembourg, 1984. 100 p.; 241 p.

This gives the most recent statistics on the main aspects of economic and social life in the regions of the community. In other words, it covers population, employment and unemployment, economic aggregates, sectors of the economy (agriculture, industry, energy, and services), education, health, and other social indicators. It also provides data on the community financial participation in investments. This is a multilingual publication.

355. Hager, Wolfgang, and Noelke, Michael. *Community—Third World: The Challenge of Interdependence.* 2d ed. Luxembourg: European Communities, 1980. 168 p. OCLC 10429667.

This study analyzes and measures the main elements of the interdependence which binds Europe and the third world together: energy; agriculture and mineral raw materials; the growing importance of the third world as an export market for the community; the new international division of labor in the manufacturing sector; financial transfer; etc. This book is a very useful source of information and provides food for thought on development problems and international cooperation.

356. Roman, Jean-Claude. *The Main Indicators of Economic Accounts in the EC, the United States and Japan, 1970–1983.* Luxembourg, 1985. 87 p. OCLC 12589529.

This shows the main indicators of national accounts for each member state of the community from 1970 to 1982. These statistics provide an indication of the principal economic trends of the community, and a comparison with the U.S. and Japan. Each statistical table is followed by an economic analysis of the figures and methodological comments which make the understanding of their conceptual meaning clear.

357. United Nations. Economic Commission for Europe (ECE). *Statistical Indicators of Short Term Economic Changes in ECE Countries.* New York, 1959–. (Monthly)

The main purpose of this bulletin is to provide an up-to-date general overview of short-term economic trends in ECE countries. The indicators have been selected in consultation with the central statistical office of the countries concerned. The statistics appearing in this publication are supplied by the governments concerned with the exception of the item "International Liquidity" data which is provided by the IMF. As of January 1984, the indices have been rebased on 1980 = 100.

GREAT BRITAIN

358. Caves, Richard E., and Krause, Lawrence B., ed. *Britain's Economic Performance.* Washington, DC: Brookings Institution, 1980. 388 p. OCLC 6304094.

This is the outcome of research undertaken by a team of American and Canadian economists in collaboration with British economists. Papers were prepared and later discussed at a conference in England in 1979, and this publication contains the revised and updated versions of those papers including discussions at the seminar. This is an extensive, thorough, and analytical study of the British economy and its performance and is full of statistical information. It is a sequel to *British Economic Prospects* by Richard E. Caves (1968) which was the result of a study undertaken by a similar team of U.S. and Canadian economists.

359. Darendorf, Ralf. *On Britain.* Chicago: University of Chicago Press, 1982. 200 p. OCLC 8554329.

The author, a German-born expatriate living in London and a renowned social scientist, writes about the decline of Britain with considerable focus on its economy. Starting with the Victorian era, he analyzes its past problems from the purely economic to the fundamentally politic and then offers concrete programs for the fututre including a national forum to ponder about where the economy is going.

360. Great Britain. Central Statistical Office (CSO). *Annual Abstract of Statistics.* London: H.M. Stationery Office, 1965–. (Annual)

This is the basic statistical yearbook for the U.K. It is drawn from all published government statistics, is quite selective in its coverage, and includes a good run of years, typically eleven. The 1987 edition, like its predecessors, covers every aspect of the economic, social, and industrial life. It has 348 tables in eighteen separate chapters. Most of the data in the annual covers the years 1975 to 1985, and some include figures for the early months of 1986. It complements the *Monthly Digest of Statistics* which contains montly or quarterly data on similar subjects.

361. Great Britain. Central Statistical Office (CSO). *Economic Trends: Annual Supplement, 1987 Edition.* London: H.M. Stationery Office, 1987. 233 p.
This supplement is the essential companion to the monthly *Economic Trends,* but it is an invaluable reference work in its own right. It provides very long runs, up to thirty-five years in some cases, of the key economic indicators which are published in the monthly journal. The longer runs are annual figures, but quarterly figures for up to twenty and twenty-five years or more are provided. The present issue is the twelfth annual supplement. The aim has been to provide a balanced selection of economic series.

362. Great Britain. Central Statistical Office (CSO). *United Kingdom National Accounts.* London: H.M. Stationery Office, 1986. 124 p.
This is the principal annual publication of national account statistics and is known as the CSO blue book. It provides detailed estimates of national product, income, and expenditure for the U.K. It covers value added by industry, personal sector, companies, public corporations, central and local government, capital formation, and financial accounts. Tables contain up to twenty-two years of data. The present volume covers the calendar years 1975 through 1985, but most of the tables in section one are extended to cover 1964 to 1974.

363. Harbury, Colin, and Lipsey, Richard G. *An Introduction to the UK Economy.* London: Pittman Publishing Limited, 1983. 240 p. OCLC 9771276.
This is a superbly written book for the comprehension and appreciation of the U.K. economy. Although it is meant to be a text and is a companion to a popular British text, *An Introduction to Positive Economics* by Richard G. Lipsey (Widenfield and Nicholson, 1983), it merits consideration by its own right. The book provides details and commentary on the U.K. economy. Some of its key features are structure of the British industry; distribution of factor incomes; international trade and development; national income and balance of payments; and government economic policy. It is generously illustrated with over 100 up-to-date charts and diagrams.

364. Lee, C. H. *The British Economy since 1700: A Macroeconomic Perspective.* New York: Cambridge University Press, 1986. 297 p. OCLC 13795096.
The purpose of this study is to porvide a coherent and comprehensive explanation of the economic development of the British economy during the past three centuries, from the eighteenth century to the present day. The book is divided into four parts. Part one, "Introduction"; part two, "1700 to 1914"; part three, "20th Century"; and part four, "Conclusions." The book has twenty-six statistical tables that help explain the growth and performance of the British economy.

365. Pope, Rex, and Hoyle, Bernard, ed. *British Economic Performance: 1880–1980.* London: Croom Helm, 1985. 214 p. OCLC 11547900.
This is a collection of extracts from documents relating to British economic performance for the period mentioned. The extracts also incorporate statistics, diagrams, and simple series. It presents views on eco-

nomic performance or prospects and includes observations about the contribution to acheivment of policies pursued by governments.

366. Townsend, Peter. *Poverty in the United Kingdom: A Survey of Household Resources and Standards of Living*. Berkeley, CA: University of California Press, 1979. 1216 p. OCLC 5795541.
This is perhaps the most detailed and comprehensive study of poverty undertaken by any society. It shows the extent of poverty in the U.K. and gives an explanation for its existence. It analyzes the incidence, causes, and impact of poverty on several classes, including the rich, and on social minorities such as the elderly, unemployed, and disabled. It also examines the effects of various government programs historically. The principal source of information for this study is the national survey carried out in 1968–69 for the specific purpose of writing this book.

JAPAN

367. Allen, George Cyril. *A Short Economic History of Japan*. 4th ed. New York: St. Martin's Press, 1981. 305 p. OCLC 6196910.
This is an excellent book to understand the Japanese economic situation and development. In the first part, Japanese history is traced from the breakdown of the feudal regime in the 1860s until the beginning of the war with China in 1937. In the second part, Japan's economic progress since the Second World War through 1979 is surveyed. The subjects covered in the book include financial and industrial organization, agriculture, industrial relations, technical innovation, and economic functions of the government. Considerable statistical information is supplied.

368. *Industrial Review of Japan/1984*. Tokyo, Japan: Japan Economic Journal, 1983. 178 p.
This provides a comprehensive and in-depth assessment of the Japanese economy giving an account industry by industry. This is authored by Japanese business journalists.

369. Japan. Economic Planning Agency. *Economic Survey of Japan*. Tokyo, Japan, 1951–52–. (Annual) OCLC 1179466.
It is considered the white paper on Japanese economy. The 1983–84 survey (published July 1985) is composed of the following chapters: chapter one, "The Japanese Economy in 1983"; chapter two, "Trends in Current Account Balance and Contributing Factors"; chapter three, "Industrial Structure in Transformation"; and chapter four, "Progress in Liberalization/Internationalization of Finance." It contains over eighty statistical charts and tables.

370. Minami, Ryoshin. *The Economic Development of Japan: A Quantitative Study*. New York: St. Martin's Press, 1986. 487 p. OCLC 15139382.
In this book, the author studies the last 100 years of Japan's economic growth from the Mejii period to the present day and makes a comprehensive survey of the Japanese experience. The book consists of three main themes. First, why was Japan able to "take off" successfully to acheive

modern economic growth initially? Second, why was Japan able to acheive a more rapid rate of economic growth than were other developed countries? Third, what is the probable future of the Japanese economy? The book is full of statistical information compiled at the Hitotsubashi University Institute of Economic Research for the original Japanese edition, but it has been updated for the English edition. The translation is by Ralph Thompson and Ryoshin Minami with assistance from David Merriman. The book also appeared in Chinese, Korean, and Thai translations.

371. Patrick, Hugh, and Rosovsky, Henry, eds. *Asia's New Giant: How the Japanese Economy Works.* Washington, DC: Brookings Institution, 1976. 943 p. OCLC 1974093.
A group of leading social analysts present a comprehensive explanation of how the Japanese have managed their economy during the past twenty years, together with an assessment of Japan's present and future economic prospects. The research was directed by the two authors from Yale and Harvard, in cooperation with Saburo Okita of the Japan Economic Research Center, Kazushi Ohkawa of Hitotsubashi University, and Tsunehiko Watanabe of Osaka University. Although out of date, it still provides a useful background in understanding the remarkable economic growth and expansion of Japan.

372. Schmiegelow, Michele, ed. *Japan's Response to Crisis and Challenge in the World Economy.* Armonk, NY: M. E. Sharpe, Inc., 1986. 309 p. OCLC 14166506.
Under conditions of global economic change that are perceived as crises in all industrialized countries, Japan is considered a success. Consequently, analysis of its economy is of great interest. The analysis is made in reference to trade and capital movement because the interaction between global economic developments, domestic structures, and national policies is most evidently reflected in the balance of payments.

MIDDLE EAST

373. Council of Arab Economic Unity. *Statistical Yearbook for Arab Countries; Volume 4.* Amman, Jordan, 1981. 529 p.
This contains basic statistics concerning important economic and social aspects of the Arab countries. The book is divided into ten parts as follows: (1) Population; (2) Labor and Wages and Consumption; (3) Agriculture; (4) Industry and Energy; (5) Foreign Trade; (6) Transport Communications and Storage; (7) Economy and Finance; (8) Tourism; (9) Health Services; and (10) Education. Added to all these are several pages covering conversion rates and references. The book contains about 300 statistical tables. It is in English and Arabic.

374. Kubursi, A. A. *The Economies of the Arabian Gulf: A Statistical Sourcebook.* London: Croom Helm, 1984. 206 p. OCLC 1127035.
Although the Gulf Cooperation Council (GCC), consisting of Saudi Arabia, Kuwait, Bahrain, Qatar, Oman, and the United Arab Emirates, is not exclusively an economic association, it is perhaps the most promising effort in economic cooperation among developing countries in recent years.

Controlling over 42 percent of the world's proven reserves of crude oil, about 63 percent of the corresponding OPEC total, and about 45 percent of world oil exports, the region is of extraordinary strategic importance. Although the importance of the Gulf or GCC is obvious, the dearth of solid reliable and up-to-date statistical information on each country separately or the region as a whole is staggering. Such data are not readily available and when available are not totally accurate or reliable or up-to-date or may cover one or more of the countries but not all. This book is an attempt to fill that void.

375. Legum, Colin, ed. *Middle East Contemporary Survey.* New York: Holmes & Meier, 1978–. (Annual) OCLC 4146581.

The 1982–83 issue is the latest available, and volume seven in this series was published in 1985. This is an annual record and analysis of economic, political, military, and international developments in the Middle East and its peripheral regions. The material in this volume is arranged in two parts: the first one consists of a series of essays which study developments relating to internal issues, both regionally and internationally; and the second part comprises a country-by-country survey of each of the Middle Eastern entities excluding Tunisia, Morocco, and Algeria. Most of the essays have been researched and written by the staff of the Shiloah Center for Middle Eastern and African Studies, Tel Aviv University.

376. Mansfield, Peter. *The Middle East: A Political and Economic Survey.* 5th ed. Oxford: Oxford University Press, 1980. 579 p. OCLC 5613079.

Although economics is only part of the title, it is quite heavy in its treatment of economic conditions. It has two statistical appendixes, although somewhat out of date. Appendix one contains general data including economic indicators, and appendix two contains information about oil reserve consumption, production, revenue, and worldwide statistics.

377. *Middle East Annual Review, 1986.* Saffron Walden, England: Middle East Review, 1985. 264 p. (Annual) OCLC 14061821; 2240878.

This is based on material provided by the Economist Intelligence Unit of the U.K. As stated on the cover of the publication, it provides key facts and figures on twenty-seven economies. In addition to the statistical information, there are several chapters concerning the Middle East, in general, which is followed by country profiles for each of the twenty-seven countries in the region.

378. Omran, Abdel-Rahim. *Population in the Arab World: Problems and Prospects.* New York: U.N. Fund for Population Activities, 1980. 215 p. OCLC 6707674.

This surveys and analyzes some of the problems facing the countries of the region. It provides data on population, social and economic characteristics, fertility, urbanization, and health.

379. United Nations. Economic and Social Commission for Western Asia (ESCWA). *Compendium of Social Statistics.* Baghdad, Iraq, 1985. 173 p. OCLC 14516654.

This is the first issue of the compendium which aims at providing numerous indicators and statistical series on social and environmental changes which lend themselves to temporal and spatial comparison. The presentation falls into seven broad categories: Population, Labor Force, Education and Culture, Justice, Health, Transportation and Communication, and Food and Agriculture. This is in English and Arabic.

380. United Nations. Economic and Social Commission for Western Asia (ESCWA). *Survey of Economic and Social Development in the ECWA Region, 1985.* Baghdad, Iraq, 1986. 165 p. OCLC 8247996.

This survey is divided into four parts as follows: Global Economy, with considerable focus on the international oil market; International Trade; Economic Performance in the ESCWA Region; and Social Development. Country tables for Bahrain, Democratic Yemen, Egypt, Iraq, Jordan, Kuwait, Lebanon, Oman, Qatar, Saudi Arabia, Syria, the United Arab Emirates, and the Yemen Arab Republic are provided. Statistical tables are annexed.

U.S.S.R.

381. Bergson, Abram, and Levine, Herbert. *The Soviet Economy: Toward the Year 2000.* London: Allen & Unwin, 1983. 452 p.

This is the revised version of the proceedings of a conference held at Airlie House, Airlie, VA, October 23–25, 1985. The conference was sponsored by the National Council for Soviet and East European Research and the National Science Foundation, and its theme was long-term prospective growth of the Soviet economy. In appraising prospects, participants were asked to take as a horizon the year 2000. No literal depiction of the state of the economy in the year was expected, but the contributions shed light on the Soviet growth process.

382. Clarke, Roger A., and Matko, Dubravko J. I., ed. *Soviet Economic Facts, 1917–81.* 2d ed. New York: St. Martin's Press, 1983. 228 p. OCLC 8132505.

This compact volume contains data such as general economic facts, urban and rural population, births, deaths and marriages, national income, industrial population, and agriculture. These are taken from the whole range of statistical volumes available and are presented in a very usable manner. The authors warn though, that the figures are not directly comparable with the Western statistics because Russian statistics are computed differently, showing a marked and consistent upward bias. However, the value of the book is in the picture it gives of the Soviet economy as a whole, even if it is somewhat inflated, because of its detail that makes up the picture.

383. Marer, Paul. *Dollar GNPs of the USSR and Eastern Europe.* Baltimore, MD: Published for the World Bank by the Johns Hopkins University Press, 1985. 241 p. OCLC 12370070.

This is the main document of a World Bank research project, undertaken to assess alternative methods of computing the per capita dollar GNP levels and growth rates of centrally planned economies (CPEs), that produced a dozen reports. This report provides highly valuable insights into the problems related to the estimation and comparison of the GNPs and GNP growth rates for the CPEs. It also concludes that the official estimates of growth rates of the CPEs "tend to yield varying degrees of upward bias." Further, the study provides insights into other issues as well includes the relationship of domestic and international prices.

384. Matthews, Mervyn. *Poverty in the Soviet Union: The Life-Styles of the Underpriviledged in Recent Years.* New York: Cambridge University Press, 1986. 227 p. OCLC 13094912.

Soviet statistical handbooks do not recognize poverty as a quantifiable phenomena and provide little data that are of direct relevance to this topic. Hence a book such as this is of considerable importance in shedding light on this subject. The first chapter reviews the historical background to Soviet poverty. Chapter two takes up the matter of what socio-occupational groups were most likely to experience it. Chapter three is devoted to the essentials of the poverty lifestyle. All three chapters are factual, but the remaining ones are more conceptual than statistical. The last chapter touches upon the social mobility into and out of poverty and the degree to which poverty exists in eastern Europe and how it may be compared with that in Russia itself.

385. Organization for Economic Cooperation and Development (OECD). *Prospects for Soviet Agricultural Production and Trade.* Paris, 1983. 117 p. OCLC 10753412.

In recent years the Soviet Union has become one of the most important purchasers of agricultural commodities from OECD countries. This report examines the extent to which this is because of natural conditions or of organizational problems and provides an outlook on agricultural developments to 1990.

386. Scherer, John L., ed. *USSR Facts and Figures Annual.* Gulf Breeze, FL, 1986. 366 p.

This is the tenth volume. About a third of this book deals with the economy, demography, energy, trade, aid, and agriculture. Information sources are mentioned, and, more important, statistical information is interpreted and analyzed and the significance of some of the events pointed out to help the users.

387. *Soviet Oil, Gas, and Energy Databook.* Compiled by PetroStudies Co., Malmo, Sweden. Stavanger, Sweden: Noroil Publishing Co., 1978. 239 p. OCLC 4815271.

Although out of date, it is a useful guide to the little-explored and little-known Soviet energy data. This is the result of a literature search and an analysis of all aspects of Soviet oil and gas development by PetroStudies, an independent Swdeish-owned company.

388. United States. Central Intelligence Agency. *USSR Energy Atlas.* Washington, DC: U.S. Government Printing Office, 1985. 79 p.
This presents a wide variety of information portraying many aspects of Soviet energy. Maps, graphics, photographs, and text provide a general understanding and appreciation of the major Soviet energy sources—oil, gas, coal, and primary electricity as well as minor fuels and alternative energy sources. It uses maps and color photos to display and focus information.

389. Ziegler, Charles E. *Environmental Policy in the USSR.* Amherst, MA: University of Massachusetts Press, 1987. 195 p.
This study demonstrates that in the 80s there is more being written about the environment and more being done to protect it than at any time in Soviet history. The volume of material published in the U.S.S.R. on environmental topics is large, and only those writings that best illuminate the Soviet system have been selected and analyzed for this study.

SOUTH AMERICA

390. Barry, Tom. *The Central America Fact Book.* New York: Grove Press, 1986. 357 p. OCLC 12313840.
This presents a detailed synopsis of the current economics and politics of each Central American country. It covers the expanding role of U.S. economic aid and the IMF loan. In addition, short profiles of the seven Central American countries highlight the major events and trends in their economies and their political and social development.

391. Fraser, Peter D. *Caribbean Economic Handbook.* London: Euromonitor, 1985. 241 p. OCLC 13667718.
The book begins with an overview of the Caribbean in the world context. It then gives a regional overview which is followed by country profiles of the larger countries and a chapter on the smaller islands. It has a statistical appendix of twenty-eight tables arranged on a comparative basis so that the countries can be compared for their population size, trade, and economic performance.

392. Ghosh, Pradip K. *Developing Latin America: A Modernization Perspective.* Westport, CT: Greenwood Press, 1984. 416 p. OCLC 11468286.
Although similar in format and organization with other books in the International Development Resource Books series, it contains a large number of statistical tables and a detailed annotated bibliography. Part one of the book is primarily a reproduction of the Inter-American Development Bank publication, *Economic and Social Progress in Latin America, 1980–81.* Part two contains the usual statistical tables, part three is the subject bibliography of about 500 items, and part four is the directory of information sources.

393. Honeywell, Martin, et al. *The Poverty Brokers: The IMF and Latin America.* London: Latin America Bureau, 1983. 138 p. OCLC 10187791.

This explains the role of the IMF, examines how it works, who benefits from its operations, and shows why it is crucial to the efforts of the Western nations to resolve the present debt crisis. As the ultimate source of credit for heavily indebted third world countries, the IMF can impose onerous conditions on those nations that need its assistance. Through case studies of Peru, Jamaica, and Chile, it demonstrates that the burden of such conditions always falls most heavily on the poorest sectors of the population. It also examines proposals for reform of the IMF and the international finance system.

394. Hopkins, Jack W. D., ed. *Latin America and Caribbean Contemporary Record.* New York: Holmes & Meier, 1981–. (Annual) OCLC 11593122.

Volume four is the latest, published in 1986, and contains 1,064 pages. This volume continues the pattern established and developed in the first three volumes. Volume one is for the year 1981–82, volume two for 1982–83, and volume three for 1983–84. Each volume is divided into five parts. Part one opens with a general review of the year's events, followed by a series of signed topical essays on current issues and problems based on the editor's judgment. The topics are broad and cover military, political, religious, social, and, to an extent, economic matters. Part two is made up of country-by-country surveys focusing on economic, political, military, and social affairs. Countries are listed alphabetically within three overall categories: South America, Central America and Mexico, and the Caribbean. However, the same country may be listed in different regional sections in different volumes. Part three consists of important documents in the political, social, and economic development of the regions. Part four provides economic, social, and political data. Part five contains book abstracts and an index. In addition to economic information in part four, country-specific economic information is also found under the country-by-country survey in part two.

395. Inter-American Development Bank. *Economic and Social Progress in Latin America, 1986 Report.* Washington, DC, 1986. 446 p. OCLC 1796358.

This report continues the series published by the bank since 1961. It has four parts. Part one comprises of five chapters covering the region's recent development trends and includes subjects such as the international environment, development financing and investment, main sector performance, and economic integration. Part two covers the changing structure of the agricultural sector in Latin America, which is the special theme of this report. The third part of the report deals with recent economic trends, economic policies, and the short- and medium-term outlook in each of the twenty-five Latin American member countries of the bank. Part four is the statistical appendix.

396. Maddison, Angus, ed. *Latin America, the Caribbean, and the OECD: A Dialogue on Economic Reality and Policy Options.* Paris: OECD, 1986. 166 p. OCLC 15135349.
Since 1982, the whole of Latin America has been in deep economic crisis for which the only historical precedent was the world depression of 1929–32. The proximate cause of this situation was clearly the debt crisis. The deeper causes are more complex, vary between countries, and are controversial. All of these are examined in this book.

397. Organization of American States. *The Economy of Latin America and the Caribbean: Analysis and Interpretations Prompted by the Financial Crisis.* Washington, DC, 1984. 36 p. OCLC 12668629.
The crisis referred to in the title is the Latin America and Caribbean region's external debt, which is over $360 billion. This publication provides an analysis of the region's economy and its growth and trends, along with pertinent statistical data. The publication is a translation of *La Economia de America Latina y el Caribe.*

398. Saunders, John V. D. *Population Growth in Latin America and US National Security.* Boston: Allen & Unwin, 1986. 305 p. OCLC 13455417.
This volume deals with both population growth in Latin America and the possible consequences of this growth for the future security of the United States. The text first analyzes the demographic dimensions of the phenomenon and then considers the consequences these may have for American security. It is pointed out that the population surge in the western hemisphere would have serious political, economic, social, and strategic implications for the United States. Neither the Caribbean nor Middle and South American industries or local agriculture will be able to absorb the surplus manpower. Increasing social tensions and economic inequalities in the hemisphere would offer the Soviets an opportunity to drive a political wedge between Latin America and the United States. Another serious consequence of the population surge in Latin America would be increased immigration to the United States. This is the first time that the interrelations between national security and population growth have been systematically analyzed.

399. *Statistical Abstract of Latin America.* Los Angeles: University of California Center of Latin American Studies, 1955–. (Annual, Irregular)
The Latin American nations include the twenty republics traditionally united by language, religion, and culture. This publication is a compilation of statistical data primarily on Latin America's economic, social, and political developments. The 1980 volume is volume twenty in this series and contains a guide to data and 684 tables in the following subject groups: main indicators, geographic, social, socioeconomic, economic, international, political, and development. Curiously, it also contains some information on the U.S., Canada, and the Caribbean.

400. United Nations. Economic Commission for Latin America and the Caribbean (ECLAC). *Agricultural Statistics: Caribbean Countries* Port of Spain: Trinidad and Tobago, 1984. 118 p.

This is volume six, and the data presented relate to the ten-year period, 1974–83. The report is divided into three parts as follows: part one, "Population and Rainfall"; part two, "Role and Contribution of Agriculture to the National Economy"; and part three, "Basic Agricultural Data." The book conatins about 100 statistical tables.

401. United Nations. Economic Commission for Latin America and the Caribbean (ECLAC). *Economic Panorama of Latin America, 1986.* Santiago, Chile, 1986. 82 p. OCLC 14816300.

This contains statistical tables and figures for Latin America as a whole and for Argentina, Brazil, Colombia, Chile, Mexico, Peru, Uruguay, and Venezeula. Statistical tables are preceded by texts summarizing the economic situation.

402. United Nations. Economic Commission for Latin America and the Caribbean (ECLAC). *Economic Survey of Latin America and the Caribbean.* Santiago, Chile, 1982–. (Annual) OCLC 9377508.

This series began in 1948 under the title *Economic Survey of Latin America* and was published from New York. It is a series of preliminary annual reports analyzing recent economic trends in individual Latin American countries. Each report presents detailed economic indicators including GDP by sector, agricultural and industrial production by commodity, foreign trade, public and private sector finances, and prices. The 1984 survey, published in 1986 is in two volumes. Volume one has two parts as follows: part one, "The Evolution of the Latin American Economy in 1984," and part two, "The Economic Evolution by Countries." Volume two is also in two parts: part one, "Trends in the Caribbean Countries," and part two, "Economic Evolution of the Individual Countries." This set, as the earlier ones, is highly informative and thorough in its treatment of the subject.

UNITED STATES

Agriculture

403. United States. Bureau of Reclamation. *1984 Summary Statistics.* Denver, CO: Division of Water and Land Technical Services, Bureau of Reclamation, 1984?. 3 vols. OCLC 11674844.

Volume one is entitled *Water, Land, and Reclamation Data* and contains historical and 1984 data on acreage, yield, production, gross crop value, and multiple purpose functions such as municipal and industrial water service, power, recreation, and flood control. Volumes two and three are published separately on a fiscal year basis. Volume two is entitled *Finances and Physical Features* and contains cost and repayment data. Volume three, entitled *Project Data,* presents much of the data summarized in other volumes. This continuing statistical series has proven valuable in preparing economic and financial studies of reclamation projects. The information provided is often used in the settlement of disputes arising from controversies over water charges, crop damage claims, and similar operations.

404. United States. Bureau of the Census. *Census of Agriculture.* Washington, DC: U.S. Government Printing Office, 1840–. (Quinquennial).
It provides benchmark statistics for all aspects of the agricultural sector. Data are provided at the national, state, and county level. Taken every five years, information is given on farms, farming, ranching, acreage, crops, fruit and nut production, vegetables, nursery and greenhouse products, value of sales, land use, irrigation, livestock and poultry, characteristics of operator, expenditures, machinery and equipment, farm finance, etc. This agriculture census was formerly taken in the years ending with the numbers four and nine. To adjust the data collection to coincide with the economic censuses and to provide comparability, a census was taken in 1978, and from then on, it is taken in the years ending with two and seven.

405. United States. Department of Agriculture. *Agricultural Outlook.* Washington, DC: U.S. Government Printing Office, 1975–. (11/yr.) OCLC 2243568.
This is the outcome of a merger of *Demand and Price Situation* (1950–75) and *Farm Income Situation* (1966–75). It brings together and sizes up what is going on in the food and fiber economy and its major components, i.e., commodities, food/marketing firm inputs, policy, and world agriculture. It gives the latest on food and fiber and combines facts and forecasts on the agricultural economy with prime statistical indicators. The coverage is on both the U.S. and other countries. Each issue has a set format and has four sections: (1) Agricultural Economy; (2) World Agriculture and Trade; (3) Farm Income Update; and (4) General Economy. The articles are descriptive in style and incorporate charts, graphs, and tables of data.

406. United States. Department of Agriculture. *Agricultural Prices: 1985 Summary.* Washington, DC: U.S. Government Printing Office, 1986. 185 p. OCLC 4023766.
This is the twenty-seventh annual summary and contains the series of prices farmers received for commodities (namely, livestock, feed, fuels, pesticides, farm supplies, and fertilizer) sold as well as prices paid for production and services.

407. United States. Department of Agriculture. *Agricultural Statistics.* Washington, DC: U.S. Government Printing Office, 1936–. (Annual) OCLC 1773189.
Prior to 1936, the information contained in this publication was published in the statistical section of the *Yearbook of Agriculture.* It is published each year to meet the diverse need for a reliable reference source on agricultural production, supplies, consumption, facilities, costs, and returns. Its table of annual data covers a wide variety of facts in forms suited to most common use.

408. United States. Department of Agriculture. *Foreign Agricultural Trade of the United States.* Washington, DC: USDA Economic Research Service 1984–. (Annual) OCLC 12542675.
This publication summarizes current and historical data on U.S. foreign trade in agricultural production. Tables highlight commodity and country information including values, quantities, principal markets for agricultural exports, import sources, and exports through a government-financed program.

409. United States. Department of Agriculture. *Yearbook of Agriculture.* Washington, DC: U.S. Government Printing Office, 1894–. (Annual).
Title varies. An 1895 act of Congress required the Secretary of Agriculture to submit an annual report in two parts, Part one was to be a business and executive statement, and part two was to contain matters of interest in order to "instruct the farmers of the country." For years this requirement was fulfilled in one volume known as the *Agriculture Yearbook*. From 1936 to 1961, each yearly volume surveyed a particular subject. Since 1962, the yearbook has been aimed toward a lay audience as is evident in some of the titles (e.g., *Will There Be Enough Food?*, published in 1981; *Cutting Energy Costs*, published in 1980). A useful list of monographic series may be found in most standard reference sources, and many of these are still in print. The 1985 yearbook, *US Agriculture in a Global Economy: 1985,* is the eighty-fourth edition and analyzes how American agriculture interacts with the nation's economy, how it functions in the realm of international trade, and how it is affected by apparently unrelated domestic policies.

Budget

410. United States. Office of Management and Budget. *Budget of the United States Government.* Washington, DC: U.S. Government Printing Office, 1922–. (Annual) OCLC 932137.
The Budget of the United States government is published annually in a group of five documents: *The Budget of the United States Government; The Budget of the United States Government, Appendix; The Budget of the United States Government, Special Analysis; Historical Tables, Budget of the United States Government;* and *The United States Budget in Brief.* In addition, there are the *Major Themes and Additional Budget Details* and *Mid-Session Review of the Budget.* Each of these documents are listed and discussed separately.
The Budget of the United States Government is the basic budget document of the United States government. It includes the President's message to Congress, a summary of the budget, long-range projections, and economic assumptions, and federal programs by function. The budgetary process is explained in detail, and summary tables are provided for each agency of the government. This volume also includes final budget figures for the last completed fiscal year and a discussion of the differences between the actual and estimated outlays by major programs and revenues by major sources. In addition, there is a preview of future budgets. The economic assumptions and demographic trends that affect the long-range budget outlook are described and analyzed. Five-year projections of budget authority and outlays covering the coming fiscal year and the four following years are part of this forecast.

411. United States. Office of Management and Budget. *Budget of the United States Government: Appendix.* Washington, DC: U.S. Government Printing Office, 1922–. (Annual) OCLC 15131 457.
This provides an in-depth look at funding for each agency's programs. This is the most detailed of all the budget documents. It provides budget estimates for each agency and schedules of permanent positions giving number of positions and salaries along with an elaborate survey of governmental activities. It has an extensive subject index.

412. United States. Office of Management and Budget. *Historical Tables, Budget of the United States Government.* Washington, DC: U.S. Government Printing Office, 1985–. (Annual) OCLC 11657250.
This provides a wide range of data on federal government finances such as data on receipts, outlays, surpluses or deficits, and federal debt covering extended time periods, in many cases from 1940 to 1991. These are much longer time periods than those covered by similar tables in other budget documents.

413. United States. Office of Management and Budget. *Major Themes and Additional Budget Details.* Washington, DC: U.S. Government Printing Office, 1983–. (Annual) OCLC 8188893.
This is a supplemental publication to the United States Budget which is divided into broad areas, such as "Agriculture and Rural Programs," "Community Development and Economic Subsidies," and "Income Security and Health." This has ceased publication with fiscal year 1985.

414. United States. Office of Management and Budget. *Mid-Session Review of the Budget.* Washington, DC: U.S. Government Printing Office, 1983–. OCLC 10037631.
This is a review of the budget at mid-year. It provides comparisons of estimates and actual figures. Statistical tables cover such areas as budget receipts, outlays, authority, current services, and budget projections.

415. United States. Office of Management and Budget. *Special Analysis, Budget of the United States Government.* Washington, DC: U.S. Government Printing Office, 1971–72–.
This provides several different views of the budget. It also looks at the impact of the budget on the entire economy in terms of the national debt, federal employment, aid to state and local governments, and national income tax policy.

416. United States. Office of Management and Budget. *The United States Budget in Brief.* Washington, DC: U.S. Government Printing Office, 1982–. (Annual) OCLC 8560802.
This is an abridged version of the budget. Its concise format and nontechnical explanations are designed to inform members of the general public about the financial performance of the federal government.

Economic Indicators and the Economy

417. Agnew, John. *The United States in the World Economy: A Regional Geography.* New York: Cambridge University Press, 1987. 264 p.

It is a textbook survey of the rise of the United States within the world economy and the causes of its relative decline. With the U.S. being the dominant state in the contemporary world scene, it is vital to understand how it got where it is today and how it is responding to the current global economic crisis. This book traces the historical evolution of the U.S. within the world economy and assesses the contemporary impact of the world economy upon and within it.

418. *America's Economy: Opposing Viewpoints-Sources.* Bruno Leone, Executive Editor. St. Paul, MN: Greenhaven Press, 1986. 453+ p.

The purpose of this Opposing Viewpoints-Sources publications is stated to present balanced, and often difficult to find, opposing points of view on complex and sensitive issues. In this anthology, diverse materials have been taken from magazines, journals, books, and newspapers, as well as from statement and position papers from a wide range of individuals, organizations, and governments. Some of the chapter topics are: World Debt Crisis, Budget Deficit, Male/Female Economics, Social Security, Welfare, Labor, and Trade. Opposing viewpoints, and a wide range of them, are placed back to back to create a running debate. This is informative, provocative, and a good orientation on the American economy. This is volume one, and a supplement of twenty-five opposing viewpoints is planned to be added each year.

419. National Planning Association. Center for Economic Projections. *Basic Maps of the US Economy, 1967–1990: Population, Employment, Income.* Washington, DC, 1979. 292 p. OCLC 6531262.

The book is divided into two parts: part one, "States"; and part two, "Economic Areas" as defined by the U.S. Bureau of Economic Analysis. Part one details economic and demographic developments at the state level. In part two, this information is charted for economic areas as mentioned before, comprising smaller and more self-contained economic entities. Within each part, the maps are grouped under four subjects: growth summaries, population characteristics, employment composition, and income by source. The maps in this volume illustrate the basic structural characteristics of the American economy and major geographic changes over time in population, employment, and income. They include historical data for the 1967–79 period and projected changes for the 1979–90 period. Statistical data used to draw each map are presented in tabular form on the facing page.

420. United States. Advisory Committee on Gross National Product Data Improvment. *Gross National Product Data Improvment Data Report.* Washington, DC: U.S. Department of Commerce. Office of Federal Statistical Policy and Standards, 1979. 204 p. OCLC 5089716.

This is a landmark report and provides the first conmprehensive evaluation of the underlying data used to estimate the national income accounts. It is a valuable planning tool in developing improved programs for economic statistics in the years ahead.

421. United States. Board of Governors of the Federal Reserve System. *Annual Statstical Digest.* Washington, DC, 1971–75–. (Annual) OCLC 3308771.

This is an annual compilation of the series of financial and business statistics found in *Federal Reserve Bulletin.* This provides historical statistical data for many of the tables found in the bulletin. Thus it serves as a convenient source of U.S. economic and financial data.

422. United States. Bureau of Economic Analysis. *Business Conditions Digest.* Washington, DC: U.S. Government Printing Office, January 1972–. (Monthly) OCLC 2452279.

This presents over 300 economic indicators for assessing current business and economic conditions and future prospects. Coverage includes consumer price index, interest rate, and related topics. One admirable feature of this publication is the presentation of the major series in graphic as well as in tabular form.

423. United States. Bureau of Economic Analysis. *Business Statistics.* Washington, DC: U.S. Government Printing Office, 1951–. (Biennial) OCLC 1227582.

This is a supplement to the *Survey of Current Business.* It contains data on national income and product accounts, U.S. international transactions, business sales, expenditures, and inventories. It covers about 2,600 business and economic series. In addition to the general economic indicators, it also provides summary data for individual industries. Its collection of economic and industrial statistics in this compact publication is astounding.

424. United States. Bureau of Economic Analysis. *Handbook of Cyclical Indicators: A Supplement to Business Conditions Digest.* Washington, DC: U.S. Government Printing Office, 1977–. OCLC 3614366.

The first formal list of cyclical indicators was published by the National Bureau of Economic Research (NBER) in 1938 followed by editions in 1950, 1961, and 1967. A comprehensive review of the cyclical indicators was completed by the Bureau of Economic Analysis (BEA) in 1975 with the cooperation of NBER staff, it resulted in the 1977 issue, and the publication continues under the BEA. This handbook is a compilation of economic indicators in the *Business Conditions Digest.* It is, therefore, a collection of descriptive and numerical data on cyclical indicators and composite indexes in one volume. The cyclical indicators include the leading, lagging, and roughly coincident indicators which tell the analysts exactly where the economy is at present and where it is headed.

425. United States. Bureau of Labor Statistics. *CPI Detailed Report.* Washington, DC: U.S. Government Printing Office, 1974–. (Monthly). OCLC 2251913.

The Consumer Price Index (CPI) is a measure of the average change in prices over time in a mixed basket of goods and services. The CPI is often used as an indicator of inflation. There are now two major forms of the

CPI commonly used: CPI-U and CPI-W. The CPI-U is the Consumer Price Index for all urban consumers and is more commonly used. CPI-W is the Consumer Price Index for urban wage earners and clerical workers. The CPI *Detailed Report* includes twenty-two tables and four charts of detailed CPI information. Overall, CPI figures for all items are included as well as are indexes for specific items. Data are also included for U.S. city averages, regions such as the northeast, and cross-tabulated with population size.

426. United States. Bureau of Labor Statistics. *Economic Projections to 1990.* Washington, DC: U.S. Government Printing Office, 1982. 151 p. OCLC 8350809.
These projections are part of the ongoing program of the bureau for study of alternative patterns of economic growth. The U.S. Department of Labor, Congress, and the Congressional Budget Office use these projections for analysis about which the future demographic composition of the work force is an important consideration. In practically all states, these data provide the framework for developing state labor force projections for planning purposes.

427. United States. Bureau of the Census. *Economic Censuses.* Washington, DC: U.S. Government Printing Office, 1809–. (Quinquennial).
These censuses are a major source of facts about the structure and the functioning of the nation's economy and therefore provide information essential for government, business, industry, and the general public. These censuses are conducted every five years for those years ending in two and seven. This program includes censuses of manufactures, retail trade, wholesale trade, service industries, mineral industries, construction, and transportation industries. Each of the individual censuses mentioned here is listed separately and discussed under its appropriate entry. The principal industry groups not covered are finance, insurance, real estate, agriculture and forestry, communications, electric, gas, and sanitary services.

428. United States. Bureau of the Census. *Social Indicators III: Selected Data on Social Conditions and Trends in the United States.* Washington, DC: U.S. Government Printing Office, 1980. 585 p. OCLC 7624058.
This is a comprehensive graphic collection of statistical data describing current social and economic conditions in the United States. It covers population and the family, health and nutrition, housing, transportation, environment, income, productivity, social security, welfare, public safety, culture, and leisure. The presentation is impressive because of colorful graphs and charts depicting the statistics to provide a comprehensive picture of life in the United States.

429. United States. Congress. *Report to the Senate and House Committees on the Budget as Required by Public Law 93-344.* Washington, DC: U.S. Congressional Budget Office, 1976–. (Annual).
This is a detailed and comprehensive report and provides an analysis of the economy and also the budget. Part one reviews the current economic situation and discusses future economic trends and developments. Part two gives five-year projections of federal spending and revenue. Topics covered in part three vary, and in some annual issues, it may even be missing.

430. United States. Department of Commerce. *International Economic Indicators.* Washington, DC: U.S. Government Printing Office, 1975–. (Quarterly) OCLC 1667573.

Title varies. Originally a part of the *Overseas Business Reports*, it contains comparative economic data for the United States and its principal industrial competitors, namely, France, Germany, Italy, The Netheralnds, Japan, Canada, and the United Kingdom. The economic indicators include GNP, industrial production, industrial operating capacity utilization, ratio of savings to disposable personal income, and ratio of fixed capital to the GNP. No commodity information is given. Data emphasize value of exports and imports and trade balances. A couple of tables deal with special country groups such as the European Community, the free world, and OPEC.

431. United States. International Trade Administration. *Foreign Economic Trends and Their Implications for the United States, FET.* Washington, DC, 1968–. (Annual or semiannual. Irregular) OCLC 1786363.

This is a series, of reports on individual countries, and each issue covers one country. Using statistics and text, it analyzes the country's total economic situation and its implications for the U.S. Reports may discuss balance of trade, trade in the U.S. and other countries, specific indusrties and commodities, and opprtunities and prospects for U.S. trade. The first page of each report is a table of "Key Economic Indicators" followed by a general economic summary. The content of these reports vary slightly from country to country, but they are especially useful for analysis of the economic situation of a country. The data are collected in the countries by the U.S. Embassy officials and transmitted to the Department of State for use as background information.

432. United States. National Advisory Council on International Monetary and Financial Policies. *Annual Report to the President and to the Congress.* Washington, DC: U.S. Government Printing Office, 1973/74–. (Annual) OCLC 2241587.

This report includes an account of the U.S. participation in the IMF and the multilateral development banks, together with related data and materials concerning the operations and policies of the fund and the banks. The statistical appendix forms a significant portion of the publication and is preceded by a short, descriptive statement of the world economic setting. The statistical tables are prepared by the Bureau of Economic Analysis, U.S. Department of Commerce, in consultation with the National Advisory Council.

433. United States. President. *Economic Report of the President, Transmitted to the Congress: Together with the Annual Report of the Council of Economic Advisors.* Washington, DC: U.S. Government Printing Office, 1947–. (Annual) OCLC 1193149.

This is essentially a report from the executive branch to the Congress on the state of the economy, and it complements the executive budget. It discusses economic factors from a perspective that transcends the annual budget cycle and examines matters that the budget can influence only marginally. Also, it describes the current state of the economy more comprehensively than does the executive budget. The annual report of the

Council of Economic Advisors comprises the major portion of this publication. It discusses economic policy and outlook and economic trends of the year, and generally has over 100 pages of statistical tables on income, employment, and production. The combination of the two reports provide a summary of the progress of the economy over the past year.

Energy

434. United States. Congress. *Energy Factbook: Data on Energy Sources, Reserves, Production, Prices, Processing and Industry Structure.* Washington, DC: U.S. Government Printing Office, 1980. 809 p.
Included in this factbook is a broad-ranging selection of domestic and international energy statistics, mostly in the form of easy to read tables and graphs. The information presented was obtained from primary sources and contains the most current figures available to Congressional Research Service. All of the tables and graphs were selected to provide answers to the energy-related questions most commonly asked and to gather in one place data that are difficult to locate in general references. A significant edition to this factbook is the inclusion of both company-specific and state-specific data of particular importance to the Congress. The emphasis in this publication has been on energy information that would help Congress in its efforts to develop national energy policy.

435. United States. Energy Information Administration. *Annual Energy Outlook, 1984 with Projections to 1995.* Washington, DC: U.S. Government Printing Office, 1985. 354 p. OCLC 9587622.
It provides projections through 1995 of the consumption and supply of energy by fuel and the end-use sector. It presents updated energy production, consumption, and price projections. It also analyzes issues, technologies, and economic events that affect the nation's energy future. The coverage is the world, selected countries, and of course, the United States.

436. United States. Energy Information Administration. *Annual Energy Review.* Washington, DC: U.S. Government Printing Office, 1977–. (Annual) OCLC 9563095.
This review presents historical data on production, consumption, stocks, imports, and prices of the principal energy commodities in the U.S. Also included are data on international production of crude oil, consumption of petroleum products, stock, and production of electricity from nuclear power facilities. Most tables are accompanied by a graphic representation or chart illustrating the data. A brief summary of energy developments and a narrative overview of statistics are presented at the beginning of the report.

437. United States. Energy Information Administration. *Annual Outlook for US Electric Power, 1986.* Washington, DC: U.S. Government Printing Office, 1985. OCLC 13223671.
This provides a history and projections of U.S. electric utility markets. It includes summary information on the production of electricity, its distribution to end-use sectors, and electricity costs and prices. It also describes the ownership structure of the industry and the operations of utility systems and outlines basic electricity generating technologies.

438. United States. Energy Information Administration. *International Energy Annual.* Washington, DC: U.S. Government Printing Office, 1979–. (Annual) OCLC 7138645.

Previous title: *International Petroleum Annual.* This covers energy production by type of energy source, supply, and disposition for major energy sources, prices, and reserves. The coverage is for the U.S., the world, and the world regions. The United States and the U.S.S.R. were the leading producers of energy, and together they accounted for 43 percent of all energy produced in 1985. The principal sources of the world's primary energy were liquid fuels, (crude oil and natural gas liquids), natural gas, coal, and electricity from hydropower and nuclear power.

439. United States. Energy Information Administration. *International Energy Outlook 1985 with Projections to 1995.* Washington, DC: U.S. Government Printing Office, 1986. 52 p. OCLC 13386065.

This report presents the current Energy Information Administration assessment of the outlook for international energy markets. This assessment has previously been included in the agency's *Annual Energy Outlook.* However, as a means of making that document more readable, its scope has been reduced to address overall domestic energy markets with the international and individual fuel assessments published separately. The plan is to update this *International Energy Outlook* annually with its publication date being about one month after that of the domestic assessment in the *Annual Energy Outlook.* The projections presented in this *International Energy Outlook* reflect the agency's understanding of the world energy market and changes that are likely to evolve in the future. These projections have been updated from those in the 1984 *Annual Energy Outlook,* based on the continued downward trend in world oil prices, stronger than previously expected economic recovery in some areas of the market economies, and other changes that have occurred in the interim.

Income and Taxes

440. Tax Foundation. *Facts and Figures on Government Finance.* New York, 1941–. (Biennial)

Title varies. This provides information on taxes, expenditures, and indebtedness on all levels of government. Federal finance data and data on the operations of state and local governments are derived from publications of the U.S. Office of Management and Budget, and the U.S. Treasury Department. There is a glossary of terms used by different governmental agencies and a topical index.

441. United States. Bureau of Economic Analysis. *Local Area Personal Income: 1978–1983.* Washington, DC: U.S. Government Printing Office, 1983. 9 vols. OCLC 3622072.

This annual began with the 1969–74 edition. The current nine volume set is divided as follows: volume one, *Summary;* volume two, *New England Region;* volume three, *Mideast Region;* volume four, *Great Lakes Region;* volume five, *Plains Region;* volume six, *Southeast Region;* volume seven, *Southwest Region;* volume eight, *Rocky Mountain Regions;* and volume nine, *Far West Region Including Alaska and Hawaii.* This set presents for local areas, the bureau's estimates of total and per capita personal income for 1978 to 1983 as well as additional detail on the sources of personal income by type and major industry. These volumes present much more than the information found in the *Survey of Current Business* which annually publishes three years of estimates of total and per capita personal income for local areas. Volume one is a national volume presenting estimates for the United States as a whole and for all the regions, states, and SMSAs. Each of volumes two to nine presents estimates for one of the eight Bureau of Analysis's regions as noted. The estimates in these volumes constitute one of the most extensive bodies of annual economic information that is available for the nation's counties and metropolitan areas.

442. United States. Internal Revenue Service. *Statistics of Income: Corporation Income Tax Returns.* Washington, DC: U.S. Government Printing Office. (Annual) OCLC 2687847.

The *Statistics of Income* series is a valuable source of current data for national income and wealth studies. Because of its use of a stratified sample and limitations resulting from the organization of quantitative data in tax returns, all qulaifying descriptions and footnotes regarding data need be carefully reviewed before use. The *Statistics of Income: Corporation Income Tax Returns* contains data by industry on assets, liabilities, receipts, deductions, net income, income subject to tax credit, distribution to stockholders, and additional tax preferences based on a sample of balance sheet and income statement statistics. Data are also classified by size of total assets and by size of business receipts.

443. United States. Internal Revenue Service. *Statistics of Income: Individual Income Tax Returns.* Washington, DC: U.S. Government Printing Office, 1954–. (Annual) OCLC 2688571.

This report contains data on sources of income, adjusted gross income, exemptions, deductions, taxable income, income tax, tax credits, self-employment tax, tax withheld, and tax payments.

444. United States. Internal Revenue Service. *Statistics of Income: International Income and Taxes, Foreign Income and Taxes Reported on US Income Tax Returns, 1976–1979.* Washington, DC: U.S. Government Printing Office, 1982. 419 p. OCLC 9636330.

This presents data on the foreign income and taxes reported by both individuals and corporations. Data are presented both for individuals claiming a deduction from all exclusion of income earned abroad and for those claiming a foreign tax credit. These data are classified by size of adjusted gross income and other criteria. Data are also presented for the Controlled Foreign Corporations of U.S. Cororations with total assets of $250 million or more. The major emphasis is the classification of the earnings, taxes, and transactions of the Controlled Foreign Corporation by the industry of both the domestic parent and the foreign corporation as well as the country of incorporation and the principal place of business of the foreign corporation.

445. United States. Internal Revenue Service. *Statistics of Income: Partnership Returns.* Washington, DC: U.S. Government Printing Office, 1977–. (Annual) OCLC 7629528.

This presents data by industry on receipts, costs of sales and operations, deductions, net income, capital gains, payments to retirement plans, and number of limited partnerships. Classifications are by state, number of partners, and by size of business receipts and size of total assets.

446. United States. Internal Revenue Service. *Statistics of Income: Sole Proprietorship Returns, 1981.* Washington, DC: U.S. Government Printing Office, 1983. 59 p. OCLC 7538626.

This contains statistics on sole proprietorships principally for income year 1981. It also contains selected statistics for income years 1957 through 1980. Data on receipts, cost of sales and operations, deductions, and net income and deficit are included. Classifications in the publication are by state and by industries for businesses with or without net income.

Industries

447. Eckstein, Otto, et al. *The DRI Report on US Manufacturing Industries.* New York: McGraw-Hill, 1984. 196 p. OCLC 11194487.

Nine leading American companies approached Data Resources Inc. (DRI) to undertake a detailed factual study of the pattern and causes of the decline of U.S. manufacturing industries and to devise an analysis that would help to explain the situation and survey available policy options. The result has been this definitive study which focuses on data and generally avoids simple explanations. The appendix provides an industry-by-industry analysis.

448. United States. Bureau of the Census. *Annual Survey of Manufactures, 1985.* Washington, DC: U.S. Government Printing Office, 1985. (Annual) OCLC 6018145.

This provides a sample survey during the intervening years between the Quinquennial Census of Manufactures which provides a complete and comprehensive survey. The 1985 Annual Survey is the thirtieth in this series. It provides the key measures of manufacturing activity for industry groups and important industries.

449. United States. Bureau of the Census. *Census of Construction Industries.* Washington, DC: U.S. Government Printing Office, 1967–. (Quinquennial) OCLC 9620630.

This provides benchmark statistics for all aspects of the construction and contracting sector including real estate developers. The following are the kind of statistics included in this report: number of construction establishments, receipts, employment, payrolls, payments for materials and for renting equipment. Capital expenditure and depreciable asssets. The bureau also publishes a number of series of construction reports such as *Housing Completions* (Monthly) and *Housing Starts* with data for states, selected Standard Metropolitan Statistical Areas (SMSAs). These various reports that make up these surveys provide a wealth of vital information on the state of the U.S. economy.

450. United States. Bureau of the Census. *Census of Manufactures.* Washington, DC: U.S. Government Printing Office, 1904–. (Quinquennial).

This was decennial from 1810 to 1900, biennial for most of the early 1900s (with certain omissions), and quinquennial from 1967. This is the main source of current data on the nation's manufacturing industries in every state, including for each number of establishments, employment, payrolls, hours worked, value added by manufacturing, quantity and value of products shipped, materials consumed, and expenditures for new plants and equipments. This is a primary source on the structure and functioning of the United States economy. In the years between each census, the bureau publishes an *Annual Survey of Manufactures* which gives census-type current data on the nation's manufacturing industry. The 1982 census (latest) is the thirty-first census of manufactures of the United States and had a universe of apporximately 345,000 establishments.

451. United States. Bureau of the Census. *Census of Service Industries.* Washington, DC: U.S. Government Printing Office, 1972–. (Quinquennial) OCLC 12372922.

This was formerly part of *Census of Business.* This series presents data for service establishments of firms subject to Federal Income Tax, and also those exempt from it. In other words, it covers all aspects of the service sector such as hotels, laundries, automotive services, amusement and recreation services, law firms, engineering firms, miscellanous repair services, personal and business services, health and social services, selected educational serivces, selected membership organizations, and non-commercial museums. Data supplied includes kinds of businesses, number of establishments, receipts and revenues, payroll, employment, size, legal form of organization, and special subjects.

Labor, Employment, and Wages

452. United States. Bureau of Labor Statistics. *Area Wage Surveys.* Washington, DC: U.S. Government Printing Office, 1950–. (Annual) OCLC 1285592.

This is a series of reports on approximately seventy individual Standard Metropolitan Statistical Areas (SMSAs) that gives average earnings for a selected group of clerical, professional and technical, skilled maintainance, and unskilled plant occupations. Each year, after all individual area wage surveys have been completed, two summary reports are issued. The first brings together data for each metropolitan area surveyed. The second presents national and regional estimates projected from individual metro-politan area data. A major consideration in the area wage survey program is the need to describe the level of movement of wages in a variety of labor markets. This program develops information that may be used for many purposes including wage and salary administration, collective bar-gaining, and determining plant location.

453. United States. Bureau of Labor Statistics. *Bargaining Calendar.* Washington, DC: U.S. Government Printing Office, 1978–. (Annual) OCLC 4763148.
This presents information assembled by the bureau on anticipated labor-management contract developments in the coming year. The information relates to major bargaining situations in which contracts expire or are subject to reopening or in which wages are subject to change. Contract developments or the results of bargaining can have a ripple effect on the economy.

454. United States. Bureau of Labor Statistics. *Employment and Wages, Annual Average: 1984.* Washington, DC: U.S. Government Printing Office, 1985. 524 p. (Annual) OCLC 9269459.
This publication is usually one or more years behind in publication; the 1984 report was published in 1985. The data contained in this report represent the complete count of employment and wages for workers covered by unemployment programs during 1984 in the fifty states and the District of Columbia. It contains national total for eleven broad industry divisions, eighty-four major industry groups, and almost all of the 1,005 four-digit SIC industries. The statistics in this publication are compiled from the quarterly tax reports submitted to state employment security agencies by employers subject to state unemployment insurance laws and federal agencies subject to unemployment compensation for Federal Employees Program. Each quarter, the state agencies compile the data and send the reports to the bureau. Data presented in this publication are by industry, state, and ownership and include the average number of reporting units, average employment, total wages, and annual average weekly wages per employee.

455. United States. Bureau of Labor Statistics. *Employment Projections for 1995.* Washington, DC: U.S. Government Printing Office, 1984. OCLC 10770486.
This presents the bureau's latest employment projections for the year 1995. It includes economic and labor force estimates on total employment, employment by industry and occupation, unemployment rate, and job growth.

456. United States. Bureau of Labor Statistics. *Geographic Profile of Employment and Unemployment.* Washington, DC: U.S. Government Printing Office, 1971–. (Annual)
This provides the widest variety of statistics for states and areas on employment and unemployment. In a single volume, this gives a complete picture of the labor force in four census regions and nine divisions, each of the fifty states and the District of Columbia, thirty metropolitan areas, and eleven central cities. It is a current source of information on demographic and economic charcteristics for metropolitan areas and cities. The data reported are labor force status by sex, race, age, Hispanic origin, marital status, occupation, industry, full- and part-time status, reasons for and duration of unemployment, and reasons for part-time work.

457. United States. Bureau of Labor Statistics. *Industry Wage Surveys.* Washington, DC: U.S. Government Printing Office, 1950–.
This covers approximately forty manufacturing and twenty-five nonmanufacturing industries. Each industry is featured about once every five years. Average hourly and/or weekly earnings, earnings distribution, occupational earning, and benefits for selected industries are given.

458. United States. Bureau of Labor Statistics. *Labor Force Statistics Derived from the Current Population Survey: A Databook.* Washington, DC: U.S. Government Printing Office, 1982. 2 vols.
This is the first comprehensive historical collection of national data from the *Current Population Survey* over the years since the survey began. Most of the statistics go through the year 1981. The compilation consists of five sections. The first section contains monthly data and annual average data on the noninstitutional population; members of the armed forces; the labor force; employment and unemployment cross-classified by a number of demographic, social, and economic characteristics. The second section contains annual average data for labor force series not previously available in historical format. The third section provides special labor force data. The fourth and fifth sections contain monthly and quarterly seasonably adjusted data for over 3,000 labor force series. The data contained in these volumes are supplemented on a current basis by the monthly publications *Employment and Earnings* and the *Monthly Labor Review.*

459. United States. Bureau of Labor Statistics. *Monthly Labor Review.* Washington, DC: U.S. Government Printing Office, 1915–. (Monthly).
This is stated to be the oldest, most authoritative government journal in its field. This presents articles on employment, wages, productivity, job security, and economic growth in the United States. This is most useful for detailed statistics on employment, work stoppages, payrolls, and other labor-related topics as well as statistics on consumer and wholesale prices. The statistics presented in it are much more detailed than in the other journals published by the bureau such as *Employment and Earnings, CPI Detailed Report,* and *Current Wage Developments.*

460. United States. Bureau of Labor Statistics. *Occupational Projections and Training Data, 1982: A Statistical and Research Supplement to the 1982–83 Occupational Handbook.* Washington, DC: U.S. Government Printing Office, 1982. 123 p. OCLC 5133145.
This provides detailed statistics on current and projected occupational employment and related information on occupational demand and supply including new estimates of job openings. It presents estimates of 1980 employment and projections of 1990 employment for 670 occupations with 1980 employment of 5,000 or higher. It provides an overview of newly developed information about occupational movements in 1980 through 1981 and discusses the outlook for fifty-five detailed occupations using this new data.

461. United States. Bureau of Labor Statistics. *Productivity Measures for Selected Industries, 1954–1980.* Washington, DC: U.S. Government Printing Office, 1982. 218 p. OCLC 8681662.

This publication updates through 1980 indexes of output per employee hour and output per employee for the industries currently included in the U.S. government's productivity measurement program. For most industries, indexes are presented beginning with 1954. Indexes are presented for eight mining industries, seventy-seven manufacturing industries, eleven transportation and other industries, and seven selected service industries. These industries are not, however, representative of the U.S. industry. Therefore, these figures should not be combined to obtain an overall measure for the entire U.S. economy.

462. United States. Bureau of Labor Statistics. *Supplement to Employment and Earnings, Revised Establishment Data.* Washington, DC: U.S. Government Printing Office, 1980–. (Annual) OCLC 6967265.

Description is based on the July 1987 issue. This annual supplement to the monthly publication *Employment and Earnings* presents revised data from the survey of establishments. This presents revised detailed industry statistics on the nation's nonagricultural workers adjusted to March 1986 benchmarks. Included are monthly and annual average employment from January 1983 to February 1987 for all employees including women, production workers in manufacturing and mining, construction workers, and nonsupervisory workers in the remaining private nonagricultural industries. Average weekly overtime hours and average hourly earnings are presented for selected manufacturing industry.

463. United States. Congress. *Current Salary Schedules of Federal Officers and Employees Together with a History of Salary and Retirement Annuity Adjustments.* Washington, DC: U.S. Government Printing Office, 1985. OCLC 2712417.

It contains current salary tables for general schedule, senior executive service, Department of Medicine and Surgery of the Veterans' Administration, foreign service, postal service employees, and executive, legislative, and judicial salaries. It also includes a history of salary adjustments for the President and Vice President; cabinet officers, members and officers of Congress, federal judges, and other employees.

464. United States. Economic Development Administration. *Annual Report.* Washington, DC, 1966–. (Annual) OCLC 1179718.

The legislative mandate of the Economic Development Administration (EDA) is to generate jobs, help protect existing jobs in economically distressed areas, and promote the capacity of states and localities to plan and conduct economic development programs. The agency has continued to provide financial assistance to economically distressed areas in the nation through a combination of public works grants, technical assistance, and guaranteed business loans.

This report discusses the activities and programs of the EDA and provides statistics for unemployment, planning, technical assistance, public works, economic adjustment, and business loans. Statistical tables summarize the different types of projects by category, state, source of financing, and type of loan.

465. United States. National Labor Relations Board. *Annual Report.* Washington, DC: U.S. Government Printing Office, 1936–. (Annual) OCLC 1606614.

The National Labor Relations Board (NLRB) is an independent federal agency created in 1935 by Congress to administer the basic law governing relations between labor unions and business enterprises engaged in interstate commerce. In its statutory assignment, the NLRB has two principal functions: (1) to determine and implement the free democratic choice by employees regarding whether they wish to be represented by a union in dealing with their employers and, if so, by which union, and (2) to prevent and remedy unlawful acts, known as unfair labor practices, by either employers or unions or both.

This report describes the activities of the board during the previous year, highlights the NLRB's case activity and effect of arbitration proceedings, and discusses different aspects of its activities including handling of unfair labor practices. It contains statistical tables.

Mines and Minerals

466. United States. Bureau of Mines. *Mineral Commodity Summaries, 1987: An Up-to-Date Summary of 88 Nonfuel Mineral Commodities.* Washington, DC: U.S. Government Printing Office, 1987. 189 p. OCLC 15147166.

This report is the earliest government publication to furnish estimates covering 1986 nonfuel mineral industry data. These data sheets contain information on the domestic industry structure, government programs, tariffs, and five-year salient statistics for eighty-eight minerals and metals in alphabetical order. The role of nonfuel minerals in the U.S. as well as in the world economy is portrayed.

467. United States. Bureau of Mines. *Minerals Yearbooks.* Washington, DC: U.S. Government Printing Office, 1932–. (Annual) OCLC 1847412.

Previous title *Mineral Resources of the United States* (1882–1931). This is a standard source of information on mineral commodities. Three volumes are published each year: volume one, *Metals and Minerals*; volume two, *Area Reports: Domestic*; and volume three, *Area Reports: International*. Volume one contains chapters on all metals and nonfuel minerals and gases that are important to the U.S. economy. The discussion and statistics for each include production, consumption and uses, stocks, prices, foreign trade, world review, and technology. Volume two covers the mineral industries of each of the fifty states, the United States island possessions in the Pacific Ocean, the Caribbean and the commonwealth of Puerto Rico. Volume three contains the latest available mineral data on more than 130 foreign countries and discusses the importance of minerals in the economies of these nations. A separate chapter reviews minerals in general and their relation to the world economy.

468. United States. Bureau of the Census. *Census of Mineral Industries.* Washington, DC: U.S. Government Printing Office, 1954–. (Quinquennial) OCLC 12129911.

This provides detailed economic statitsics for all aspects of the mineral industry sector. The mineral industries in recent years have accounted for about 2 percent of national income and have provided employment for about 1 percent of all gainful workers in the United States. Nevertheless, the mineral industries furnished a large proportion of the raw materials base of the economy. In 1982, the mining industries accounted for 40 percent of the net value added by the combined domestic raw materials industries of mining, agriculture, forestry, and fishing.

Population, Housing, and Vital Statistics

469. United States. Bureau of the Census. *Census.* Washignton, DC: U.S. Government Printing Office, 1790–.

The first U.S. census was taken in 1790 as provided in the Constitution shortly after the nation came into being. Since then, the country has regularly counted its people; their activities, products, and possessions; and has noted the changes taking place over time. In a census, the bureau counts and classifies every person, household, housing unit, farm, mine, factory, business, or government in the area where the census is being taken, which could be the nation as a whole, a single city, or a particular type of activity. Some censuses are taken every five years, but others occur every ten years. Federal censuses that are useful for economic information begin with the decennial *Census of Population* (1790-) and the various series of *Current Population Reports.* Others are *Agriculture* (1840-), *Housing* (1940-), *Manufactures* (1929-), *Mineral Industries* (1954-), and *Transportation* (1963-). The bureau now employs the term Economic Censuses to mean all the above except population and agriculture plus the censuses of the outlying areas and enterprise statistics. Each of the individual censuses mentioned above is listed and discussed under its appropriate entry.

470. United States. Bureau of the Census. *Census of Housing.* Washington, DC: U.S. Government Printing Office, 1940–. (Decennial) OCLC 7463372.

Housing statistics are one indicator of the nation's economy, and very detailed tabulation on the number and characteristics of houses are provided in this census report. The 1980 census of housing is in multiple volumes, and the three basic series are *General Housing Characteristics, Detailed Housing Characteristics,* and *Metropolitan Housing Charateristics.* Some of the typical information found in housing census reports are housing units; household type; age, race, and sex of householder; year moved in; bedrooms; year built; household income; and plumbing, heating, and rent. Information on housing value in a given area, water source, sewer availability, fuel and heating equipment, and costs and mortgage data are also provided.

471. United States. Bureau of the Census. *Census of Population.* Washington, DC: U.S. Government Printing Office, 1790–.
These census reports are issued in two main volumes: volume one, *Characteristics of the Population* and volume two, *Subject Reports.* The *1980 Census of Population*, volume one, has the following as its partial contents: Number of Inhabitants; General Population Characteristics; General Social and Economic Characteristics; and Detailed Population Characteristics. This census provides the most detailed statistics available and the most complete geographic coverage. The bureau also publishes a number of reports designed to provide demographic estimates between each decennial census. These series are called Current Population Reports which is discussed under the entry for it.

472. United States. Bureau of the Census. *Current Population Reports.* Washington, DC: U.S. Government Printing Office, 1946–. (Irregular).
For statistics more current than the latest census, this series provides more frequent data. Several reports in this series contain income data. Some of the important ones are listed below and discussed here.

Consumer Income. Data on the poroprtions of families, individuals, and households at various income levels are given. Information is also presented on the relationship of income to age, sex, race, family size, eductaion, occupation, work experience, and other characteristics. A special annual report provides detailed information on low income families and individuals.

Economic Characteristics of Households in the United States. This provides detailed data at the national level for sources of income of U.S. households.

Farm Population. Among other statistical farm information, annual population estimates for rural areas of the U.S. are given.

Population Characteristics. This is a series of reports on various charateristics of the national population, e.g., mobility, fertility, marital status, education, etc.

Population Estimates and Projections (Monthly). Annual estimates of the population of the states by broad age groups and of the United States by age, race, and sex are provided. Annual estimates of the components of the population change are also given. Estimates of the population of selected metropolitan areas are also listed.

473. United States. Bureau of the Census. *Pocket Data Book USA.* Washington, DC: U.S. Government Printing Office, 1967–. (Biennial?, Irregular) OCLC 7058811.
This is a Census Bureau compilation of facts and figures on population and vital statistics, immigration and law enforcement, income and prices, labor, manufacturing and construction, housing, mining and transportation, science and energy, finance and insurance, etc. Many tables show historical data as well as current statistics. This is a quick ready reference source.

474. United States. Department of Housing and Urban Development. *Projections of Housing Consumption in the US, 1980 to 2000, by a Cohort Method.* Washington, DC: U.S. Government Printing Office, 1980. 105 p. OCLC 7037974.

This is *Annual Housing Survey Studies* number nine. Information is provided on the number of people and families, number of households, number rented and owned, structure type, and number of rooms. A picture of the direct impact on housing of impending changes in the size and age structure of the population emerges from this presentation.

475. United States. Department of Justice. *Statistical Yearbook of the Immigration and Naturalization Service.* Washington, DC: U.S. Government Printing Office, 1978?–. (Annual) OCLC 7063193.

This is a compendium of statistics relating to immigrants broken down by about seventy different categories. Some of the categories are listed below: immigration to the United States: 1820–1980; immigration by country for decades: 1820–1980; immigrants admitted by type of admission and country or region of birth: fiscal year 1980; aliens who were adjusted to permanent resident status in the United States by country or region of birth: fiscal year 1980; and refugees admitted/adjusted to lawful permanent resident status by fiscal year 1946–1980.

476. United States. National Center for Health Statistics. *Changing Mortality Patterns, Health Services Utilization, and Health Care Expenditures: United States, 1978–2003.* Washington, DC: U.S. Government Printing Office, 1983. OCLC 9644435.

This contains basic projections for several health items. For example, life expectancy is projected by sex to 2003, and the life expectancies of different countries are compared. It also examines in detail how two alternative mortality assumptions, projected to the year 2003, affect estimates of health care utilization and expenditures in the future.

477. United States. National Center for Health Statistics. *Vital Statistics of the United States, 1982.* Washington, DC: U.S. Government Printing Office, 1986. 3 vols in 4 parts. OCLC 1168068.

This is the most comprehensive report on U.S. vital statistics published since 1937. Three annual sections are published: (1) Natality; (2) Mortality (usually in two parts); and (3) Marriage and Divorce. A geographic and subject guide to each section is included.

478. United States. Public Health Service. *Health United States.* Washington, DC: U.S. Government Printing Office, 1976–. (Annual) OCLC 3151554.

Title varies, and also every third year, it includes a third section entitled Prevention Profile. This annual presents statistics on births, deaths, abortions, fetal deaths, life expectancy, fertility, and compares and contrasts them. The 1985 issue contains twenty-one charts and 101 statistical tables covering health status and determinants, utilization of health resources, health care resources, and health care expenditures.

States and Cities

479. Burchell, Robert W., and Listokin, David. *Cities under Stress: The Fiscal Crises of Urban America.* Piscataway, NJ: The Center for Urban Policy Research. The State University of New Jersey, 1981. 723 p.
Although the focus of the book is on financial problems facing cities in the 1980s, it also covers regional economic shifts, inflation, and demographic changes. The book is a collection of invited essays that provide a foundation for the understanding of the problems that cities face in delivering adequate and regular public services to their residential populations.

480. Garwood, Alfred N., ed. *Almanac of the 50 States: Basic Data Profiles with Comparative Tables.* Burlington, VT: Information Publications, 1985. 446 p. OCLC 11719548.
It is a comprehensive and easy-to-use reference book for the states. It presents a general statistical overview of every state along with tables of comparative ranking. The volume is divided into two parts. Fifty-two eight-page profiles, organized into thirteen subject categories, one for each of the states and the District of Columbia, and a U.S. summary make up the first part of this volume. The second part of the volume consists of tables which provide objective rankings of the states for fifty-two characteristics including population, vital statistics, energy consumption, civilian labor force, unemployment rate, average hourly or weekly earnings, etc. On the whole, this is indeed an excellent compilation, compact and convenient to use.

481. Garwood, Alfred N. *199 American Cities Compared: Basic Data Profiles for the Nation's Largest Cities.* Burlington, VT: Information Publications, 1984. 216 p. OCLC 10486407.
This is also a comprehensive and easy-to-use reference source. It is a statistical portrait of the nation's largest cities, and collectively, it depicts a picture of the country's most significant urban centers. Every city profile contains sixty-two items of information, and it is heavy on demographic and economic information. Because the format is the same for all the cities and there is uniformity and consistency of content, comparison between cities is easy.

482. Marlin, John Tepper. *The Book of American City Rankings.* New York: Facts on File, 1983. 371 p.
The book contains 267 tables with information on life in America's 100 largest cities where 22 percent of Americans live. Accompanied by interpretative texts, the tables allow the reader to compare and rank the diverse characteristics of these cities. In the second part of the book, the rankings for each city have been summarized to assist in further evaluation of each individual city.

483. *New York State Statistical Yearbook.* Albany, NY: New York State Division of the Budget. 1968–. (Annual, Irregular) OCLC 1923453.
This yearbook is designed to facilitate access to an extensive range of information about the Empire State and the widley diverse characteristics of its residence, economy, geography, governmental programs, and finance. It contains significant narrative information as well as numerous statistical

tables grouped according to broad functional areas. For the reader's conve-
nience, each section has four introductory pages. One page provides a
listing, by number and title, of all tables and charts within that section. On
another page are "User Notes" which direct the reader to additional
sources of related information or describe unique situations that may affect
the availability or nature of certain data.

484. *State Demographics: Population Profiles of the 50 States.* Prepared
by the American Demographics Magazine Editors. Homewood, IL:
Dow Jones-Irwin, 1984. 335 p. OCLC 10219301.
This handbook presents information for the U.S., the four census regions,
the fifty states, and the District of Columbia. In addition to basic data on
population and households, valuable statistics on income, occupation and
employment, housing, education, etc., are supplied. The states are listed
alphabetically, with comparable census data given for each one. For each
date a map shows the major geographic areas, a line chart shows population growth at a glance, and a population pyramid shows the age structure
according to the 1980 census. In short, in one volume, most frequently
sought census data relating to the states and regions is assembled here.

485. Terhune, Frances W., ed. *1982 Florida Statistical Abstract.* Gaines-
ville, FL: The University of Florida, Bureau of Economic and Business
Research, College of Business Administration, 1982. 712 p.
Editor varies. This is the sixteenth edition of this abstract and provides
comprehensive economic and demographic information about Florida. The
first part of the abstract includes tables that present information about the
characteristics of the population: number of people, housing, health, education, income, employment, and welfare. The next three chapters refer to
establishments engaged in economic, social, and political activities. The
last section of the book contains exhibits of a comparative nature: economic and social trends. One of the sections therein covers a number of
time series showing the fluctuations of such major economic activities as
income, prices, and employment. In another section, measures of the
quality of life in the state and metropolitan areas are given. The sources of
data are listed at the bottom of each table. Suggestions for locating sources
or obtaining more information are made at the end of the book under the
caption "Guide to Sources of Statistics."

486. United States. Bureau of the Census. *County and City Data Book.*
Washington, DC: U.S. Government Printing Office, 1947–.
(Quinquennial, Irregular) OCLC 10612451.
This is a supplement to the *Statistical Abstract of the United States.* It is a
compact social and economic profile that provides statistics for each
county and for each city with 25,000 or more inhabitants. It also gives
information on standard federal administrative regions, census regions and
divisions, and states. The 1983 issue is the tenth in this series and contains
1,060 pages and presents the variety of information as already noted.
These statistics represent generally useful summary measures that are
available in comparable form for the geographic areas covered. For this
edition, many of the results are from the 1980 *Census of Population* and
Census of Housing and data on such subjects as labor force, income, etc.,
have been emphasized.

487. United States. Bureau of the Census. *State and Metropolitan Area Data Book.* Washington, DC: U.S. Government Printing Office, 1979–. (Annual).

This is a supplement to the *Statistical Abstract of the United States.* This compendium presents a variety of statistical information on Standard Metropolitan Statistical Areas (SMSAs), central cities of SMSAs, census regions and divisions, and states. Some of the subjects covered include area and population, households, housing, income, labor force, financing, employment, manufactures, vital statistics, and retail and local trade.

Trade

488. United States. Bureau of Industrial Economics. *Franchising in the Economy, 1981–1983.* Washington, DC, 1983. 85 p. OCLC 6035362.

Franchising as a method of distribution has become a significant part of the U.S. economy, comprising numerous categories of commercial enterprise and including all of the ingredients of the marketing system, i.e., planning, production, packaging, pricing, promotion, advertising, selling, buying, and competing. To follow this rapidly growing industry, the bureau has conducted its eleventh annual survey of franchisers, which is reported below.

This report presents summary data on franchising activity in the U.S. during 1981 by type of franchised business. Estimated data are presented for 1982 and 1983. Selected historical data are presented for each year from 1969 to 1980.

489. United States. Bureau of Labor Statistics. *Comparisons of US, German, and Japanese Export Price Indexes.* Washington, DC: U.S. Government Printing Office, 1980. 41 p. OCLC 5943933.

This report compares price changes for comparable categories of products for Germany, Japan, and the U.S. The first part deals with the methodology for calculating export price index ratios. The second part describes the data used in the construction of U.S.-Germany and U.S.-Japan export price index ratios. The last part briefly discusses the behavior of a limited number of these ratios. Thirty-four U.S.-Germany and twenty-six U.S.-Japan comparisons are made covering selected categories of industrial products. Although export price index comparisons may be either multilateral or bilateral, the ratios developed here make bilateral comparisons.

490. United States. Bureau of the Census. *Census of Business.* Washington, DC: U.S. Government Printing Office, 1929–. (Quinquennial)

It is quinquennial from 1967 on, and a complete census was taken for each of the following years: 1929, 1933, 1935, 1939, 1948, 1954, 1958, 1963, and 1967. The material is presented in multivolumes for certain years. Along with industry groupings, it covers retail and wholesale trade, service establishments, sales, employment, payroll, number of firms, number of establishments and industry groupings. In addition to national aggregates, data are summarized for states, counties, cities, and SMSAs.

491. United States. Bureau of the Census. *Census of Retail Trade.* Washignton, DC: U.S. Government Printing Office, 1972–. (Quinquennial) OCLC 11271435.

This was formerly part of *Census of Business*. This census provides benchmark statistics on all aspects of the retail sector by state, SMSA, and areas outside of SMSA for over 100 different kinds of retail enetrprises. The data include number of establishments, payroll, employment, sales, and sales by merchandise, etc. It is normally broken down into three parts: (1) geographic area series; (2) industry series; and (3) special series.

492. United States. Bureau of the Census. *Census of Wholesale Trade.* Washington, DC: U.S. Government Printing Office, 1972–. (Quinquennial) OCLC 12294791.

This was formerly part of *Census of Business*. Data are provided on number of establishments, receipts, payroll, kinds of business, sales by commodity, employment, operating expenses, inventories, legal form of organization, type of operation, and special subjects. It is in two volumes: (1) geographic area series, and (2) industry series.

493. United States. Bureau of the Census. *County Business Patterns.* Washington, DC: U.S. Government Printing Office, 1946–. (Annual) OCLC 2475762.

Title varies. Each volume is issued in several parts, the first being the U.S. summary, and each of the others covering a single state of the U.S. This is a useful annual compilation of first-quarter employment and payroll statistics by geographic area and industry. It provides data covering most of the economic divisions, such as agricultural services, mining, construction, manufacturing, transportation, public utilities, wholesale trade, retail trade, finance, insurance, real estate, and services. Summary data for the United States are presented first, followed by data at the individual state and county level.

494. United States. International Trade Administration. *Investment Climate in Foreign Countries.* Washington, DC, 1983–. 4 vols. OCLC 10127264.

The individual volumes are titled as follows: (1) *OECD and Other European Countries*; (2) *Africa*; (3) *Asia Excluding Japan*; and (4) *Western Hemisphere Excluding Canada*. Approximately every two years, U.S. embassies throughout the world prepare investment climate statements summarizing the laws, policies, and economic climate of their respective host countries which may affect existing or new direct investment. Statements include information on the condition and quality of host country infrastructure; availability of selected economic resources; and government policies in the areas of taxation, nationalization, and performance requirements imposed by host country governments.

495. United States. Office of Trade and Investment Analysis. *United States Trade Performance and Outlook, 1985.* Washington, DC: U.S. Government Printing Office, 1985. 152 p. OCLC 11094055.

This third annual report (maybe the last as indicated in a note inside back cover) presents a comprehensive analysis of U.S. trade and its role in the world economy. It describes the links among trade deficits, capital flows, and the growing U.S. international debtor position. The narrative part of the report which accounts for most of it, is liberally illustrated with charts and tables. The statistical appendix contains numerous tables on basic import and export statistics.

496. Yochelson, John N., ed. *The United States and the World Economy: Policy Alternatives for New Realities.* Boulder, CO: Westview Press, 1985. OCLC 11784979.
The structure of the world economy has changed dramatically in recent years reflecting a redefinition of U.S. interests in light of increasing foreign penetration in U.S. markets, global pressures for protectionist policies, the emergence of the newly industrializing countries, and the vulnerabilities of the international financial system. This volume contains a selection of stimulating policy papers on these and other related matters.

Transportation

497. United States. Bureau of the Census. *Census of Transportation.* Washington, DC: U.S. Government Printing Office, 1963–. OCLC 9762174.
The 1982 census is the latest and consists of three surveys: (1) Truck Inventory and Use Survey; (2) Commodity Transportation Survey; and (3) Non-Regulated Motor Carriers and Public Warehousing. These surveys were previously taken in 1967, 1972, and 1977. The Truck Inventory and Use Survey provides data on the physical and operational characteristics of the nation's truck population. It is based on a sample of 26 million registrations of private and commercial trucks. It gives number of vehicles, major use, vehicle miles, and characteristics such as body type. The Commodity Transportation Survey reports on a sampling of characteristics of inter-city commodity shipments originated by manufacturers including ton-miles, means of transport, length of haul, size of shipment, etc. Non-Regulated Motor Carries and Public Warehousing Survey has data on motor carriers that serve the public but are not subject to regulation by the Interstate Commission.

498. United States. Department of Transportation. *National Transportation Statistics: Annual Report, September 1983.* Washington, DC: U.S. Government Printing Office, 1983. 230 p.
This report is a summary of selected national transportation statistics from a wide variety of government and private sources. Included are costs, inventory, performing data, passenger and cargo operations of air carriers, general aviation, automobiles, buses, trucks, rail, water, and oil and gas pipelines. It also covers operating revenues and expenses, number of vehicles and employees, vehicle miles, and passenger miles, etc. Supplementary sections deal with energy and transportation. In this edition, the selected data cover the period 1971 through 1981–82.

499. United States. Federal Aviation Administration. *FAA Statistical Handbook of Aviation.* Washington, DC: U.S. Government Printing Office, 1959–. (Annual) OCLC 2707503.
This continues the *CAA Statistical Handbook of Civil Aviation.* The prime purpose of this publication is to serve as a convenient source for historical

data and to assist in evaluating progress. It presents statistical information pertaining to the Federal Aviation Administration, National Air Space System, airports, airport activity, U.S. Civil Air Carrier Fleet, U.S. Civil Air Carrier Operating Data, Airman, General Aviation Aircraft, Aircraft Accidents, and Imports and Exports and Aeronautical Production.

500. United States. Federal Highway Administration. *Highway Statistics.* Washington, DC: U.S. Government Printing Office, 1945-. (Annual) OCLC 1796740.

This publication brings together annual series of selected statistical tabulations relating to highway transportation in three major areas: (1) Highway Use—the ownership and operation of motor vehicles; (2) Highway Finance—the receipts and expenditures for highways by public agencies; and (3) the Highway Plant—the extent, characteristics, and performance of the public highways, roads, and streets in the nation. The fourth section deals with the financing of highways by all government agencies. The fifth section provides data on highway mileages and performance, and the sixth section gives statistics for American Samoa, Guam, the Commonwealth of Northern Marianas Islands, and Puerto Rico. The final section presents summaries from the Nationwide Personal Transportation Study.

501. United States. Interstate Commerce Commission. *Transport Statistics in the United States.* Washington, DC: U.S. Government Printing Office. OCLC 6881764.

This supercedes *Statistics of Railways in the United States.* This report is in two parts: part one, "Railroads"; part two, "Motor Carriers." This provides detailed data on traffic, operations, equipment, finances, and employment for carriers subject to the Interstate Commerce Act. The 1984 issue is the latest available.

Sources Consulted

The selections made for this bibliography are based, to a large extent, on the existing collections of the following libraries: United Nations Library System, including its satellite specialized libraries; the Joint Library of the World Bank and the International Monetary Fund Library in Washington, DC; U.S. Department of Commerce Library; New York University Elmer Holmes Bobst Library, International Documents Collection; and the St. John's University Library.

In addition to the materials from the above libraries, within the scope of this bibliography, the following printed sources were consulted for selection and verification.

502. *American Statistics Index (ASI)*. Washington, DC: Congressional Service, 1973–. (Annual). OCLC 1784446.
It is subtitled "A Comprehensive Guide and Index to the Statistical Publications of the U.S. Government." It is a comprehensive index for locating any kind of statistical publication by a U.S. government agency. Abstracts, based on examinations of the original publication, provide full bibliographic data, description, and tables. This is published in two volumes: volume one, *Index*; and volume two, *Abstract*.

503. Blauvelt, Euan, and Durlacher, Jennifer. *Sources of Asian/Pacific Economic Information*. Westport, CT: Greenwood Press, 1981. 2 vols. OCLC 7196646.
This covers the region of the world extending from the Indian subcontinent to the Pacific Islands. It consists of two volumes containing in all more than 5,000 entries, with annotations which are mostly brief. Each volume contains roughly half the sources with the international sources at the beginning of volume one. Each volume concludes with two indexes. The first lists all the sources alphabetically, irrespective of the country of coverage. The second provides a subject breakdown. Sources are listed by subject within the country covered.

504. Blauvelt, Euan, and Durlacher, Jennifer. *Sources of European Economic Information*. 4th ed. Westmead, England: Gower Publishing Co., 1983. 643 p. OCLC 9387737.
It contains about 6,000 entries and covers eastern as well as western Europe. Part one of the book lists information sources with brief annotations. Part two presents the full name and address and other available necessary details of the issuing agencies. The volume concludes with two

indexes. The first lists all the sources alphabetically, the second provides a subject breakdown. The publication is indeed extensive.

505. Brown, Barbara E., ed. *Canadian Business and Economics: A Guide to Sources of Information.* Ottawa, ON: Canadian Library Association, 1984. 469 p. OCLC 11813365.

This is a guide to over 6,500 governmental and nongovernmental publications relating to Canadian business and economics. Only materials with Canadian emphasis and published in Canada have been included. Statistical publications from Statistics Canada have generally been excluded with the exception of those of general interest. Publications considered no longer useful or directories more than five years old have also been excluded. The index is a dictionary index in two languages. The entries are in English or French with the description given in the language of the entry, and bilingual items are listed in both languages. The title of this bibliography is also in French.

506. Conference Board. *Cumulative Index, 1986.* New York, 1986. 54 p.

The Conference Board, based in New York, is a business information service whose purpose is to assist senior executives and other leaders in arriving at sound decisions. Since its foudning in 1916, the board has been creating close personal networks of leaders who exchange experience and judgment on significant issues in economics, public policy, and management practice. The networks are supported by an international program of research and meetings which the Conference Board staff of more than 350 persons carries out from offices in New York, Ottawa, and Brussels. More than 3,600 organizations in over fifty nations participate in the board's work as Associates. It is a not-for-profit corporation and the large share of its financial support comes from business concerns, many with worldwide operations.

The index is an annually revised guide to the board's publications. It covers a wide range of studies, pamphlets and articles in the areas of economic and policy analysis, consumer research, international business management, and human resources. It has a useful subject index. The board's publications are of inestimable value to business and economics, and these are generally considered to be thoroughly professional.

507. Daniells, Lorna M. *Business Information Sources.* rev. ed. Berkeley, CA: University of California Press, 1985. 673 p. OCLC 10696150.

This is an outstanding work in this field. It has a number of citations listed under "Economic Conditions" in the index. There are other publications of interest listed elsewhere.

508. Dicks, G. R., ed. *Sources of World Financial and Banking Information.* Westmead, England: Gower Publishing Co., 1981. 720 p. OCLC 7548300.

The directory is organized in three parts. In part one, nearly 5,000 sources of data, comment, and interpretation of a financial, banking, or economic nature are put together. The material is arranged alphabetically by country, and where a source covers a number of countries, it appears in the international section at the beginning of the book. Part two gives further details on the issuing bodies listed in part one. Part three presents the basic source material in a seven-part index. The sections are general economic and financial information; national income accounts and public finance; money and banking; companies and stocks and shares; households and persons; balance of payments and energy; and prices. It is indeed an impressive undertaking.

509. Fletcher, John, ed. *Information Sources in Economics.* 2d ed. Boston: Butterworth's 1984. 339 p. OCLC 10230826.

It is a survey of, and guide to, the wide range of sources of information used by economists. It is prepared by twenty-two British librarians and economists and is in twenty-four chapters. First are two chapters on economics libraries and how to search for relevant economic information. Then follow eight chapters on particular types of economics literature including statistical sources, official publications of the U.K. and U.S. governments, and international organizations. The remaining chapters review information sources and literature of a specialized economics subject.

510. Ganly, John, and Sciattara, Diane M., ed. *Serials for Libraries: An Annotated Guide to Continuations, Annuals, Yearbooks, Almanacs, Transactions, Proceedings, Directories, Services.* 2d ed. New York: Neal-Schuman Publishers, 1985. 441 p. OCLC 11917960.

Included in it are English-language titles which are available in the United States, published on an annual or other continuing basis, but no more than once a year, and are suitable for collection by public school, academic, and special libraries. On a limited basis, important multilanguage titles and publications by U.N. and other agencies are included. The selections are excellent, and the annotations are useful. Economics and related subjects are widely represented.

511. Harvey, Joan M. *Statistics Africa: Sources for Social, Economic, and Market Research.* 2d ed. Beckenham, England: CBD Research, 1978. OCLC 4667269.

This is a guide to sources of statistics in Africa and adjacent islands. Like its companion volumes, the arrangement is first in alphabetical order by country and then, within each country, by the subject of the statistics under standard groups: general production; external trade; internal distribution; population; social; finance; transport; and communications. Subject, title and organization indexes are included.

512. Harvey, Joan M. *Statistics America: Sources for Social, Economic and Market Research.* 2d ed, rev. and enlarged. Beckenham, England: CBD Research, 1980. 385 p. OCLC 7330361.

This is a guide covering sources of statistics on North, Central, and South America. It is also arranged alphabetically by country, and major statistical sources are listed under the standard groups as listed in the previous citation. Subject, title, and organization indexes are provided.

513. Harvey, Joan M. *Statistics Europe: Sources for Social, Ecoonmic, and Market Research.* 4th ed. Beckenham, England: CBD Research, 1981. 508 p. OCLC 8037388.

This is a compilation of sources of statistics for western and eastern Europe published by the countries themselves and by the organizations such as the U.N., the OECD, the EC, and others. Statistical sources for the whole continent are at the front of the volume. It is followed by country listings arranged alphabetically under the standard groups mentioned under the previous citations. It also has author, title, and organization index.

514. Hoel, Arline Alchian; Clarkson, Kenneth W.; and Miller, Roger LeRoy. *Economics Sourcebook of Government Statistics.* Lexington, MA: Lexington Books, 1983. 271 p. OCLC 9536089.

This is a compilation of the main economic indicators put out by the U.S. government agencies. Over fifty economic statistics are explained and described. It includes what they are, what they are based on, what their potential limitations are, when they are released, etc. The indicators are categorized by type into six categories: measures of inflation; profits—indicators of general business conditions; interest rates and other financial indicators; measures of employment, unemployent, and earnings; indicators of international finance and trade; and indicators of government influence. The presentation is in nontechnical terms.

515. Hoopes, David S., and Hoopes, Kathleen R. *The Global Guide to the World of Business.* New York: Facts on File, 1983. 847 p. OCLC 7248520

As stated in the introduction, this is meant to be a first-stop reference point for persons with any question about practical aspects of any phase of international business operations. The major part of the book is a selected, descriptive list by country and sources of information about that country. This is preceded by sources of general information on international business and regional information.

516. Marsden, David, and Redlbacher, Lydia. *A Guide to Current Sources of Wage Statistics in the European Community.* Washington, DC: European Community Information Service, 1984. 169 p. OCLC 12081857.

This is a book of wage statistics sources broken down by EC member countries. It also comprises accounts of methods used in wage statistics in the European Community. Information about the sources are descriptive allowing for comparisons of pay trends and structures between different member countries.

517. Marshall, Joan K., comp. *Serials for Libraries: An Annotated Guide to Continuations, Annuals, Yearbooks, Almanacs, Transactions, Proceedings, Directories, Services.* New York: Neal/Schuman Publishers, 1979. 494 p. OCLC 5339204.

It is a selection of about 2,000 serial titles considered important for libraries. It is limited to English-language publications.

518. Mayros, Van, and Werner, D. Michael. *Business Information: Applications and Sources.* Radnor, PA: Chilton, 1983. 490 p. OCLC 9323344.

It is a guide that will enable a company to identify both its information needs and those sources that should be accessed to create an on-going information retrieval system. A list of ten general business areas in the form of chapters is developed in the first section of the book entitled

"Applications." From this list, 113 specialties, grouped as subchapters, are generated. Each subchapter begins with a description of the types of information available in the sources and a suggested list of typical applications given. In addition to citing sources under each subchapter, there is a second section of the book called "Sources." The sources themselves are of six types including general reference, periodical sources, information brokers, etc. Besides listing over 3,800 sources of information, it also demonstrates the potential uses of these sources. Listing of two other companion volumes follow.

519. Mayros, Van, and Werner, D. Michael. *Guide to Information from Government Sources.* Radnor, PA: Chilton, 1983. 188 p. OCLC 9576017.

Like the other two companion volumes, this is also divided into two major sections: "Applications" and "Sources." In the first section, each of the ten chapters deal with a specific area within business. Each chapter is further subdivided into subchapters focusing on a specific topic. Each subchapter is introduced with a description which explains the types of information to be found in the information sources listed in the section. Next, a list of sample applications depicting how the related sources can be used is given.

520. Mayros, Van, and Werner, D. Michael. *Information Sourcebook for Marketers and Strategic Planners.* Radnor, PA: Chilton, 1983. 326 p. OCLC 9620024.

Like the other companion volumes, this is also divided into two parts: "Applications" and "Sources." It lists about 2,500 annotated sources from government agencies as well as from private publishers. As is true of the other two volumes, this is also an annotated bibliography and describes and demonstrates by examples the potential use of the sources listed.

521. Moore, Geoffrey Hoyt, and Moore, Melita H. *International Economic Indicators: A Sourcebook.* Westport, CT: Greenwood Press, 1985. 373 p. OCLC 11114228.

This provides detailed information on the international economic indicators that have been selected and compiled by the Center for International Business Cycle Research at Columbia University Business School. The function of international economic indicators is explained in the introductory chapter. It covers the seven largest industrial countries: the U.S., U.K., Canada, West Germany, France, Italy, and Japan. It contains a helpful "Indicator Series Finding Guide" at the end.

522. Mossman, Jennifer. *Encyclopedia of Geographic Information Sources: US Volume.* 4th ed. Detroit, MI: Gale Research, 1986. 437 p. OCLC 13796415.

It covers more than 390 geographical locations giving available reference sources about each. Organized by counties, cities, and states, the materials are grouped under statistical sources, periodicals, abstracts, and indexes. A special section called "Multinational Publications" lists sources that are multigeographical.

523. O'Brien, Jacqueline Wasserman, and Wasserman, Steven R. *Statistics Sources.* 10th ed. Detroit, MI: Gale Research, 1986. 2 vols. OCLC 13378143.

From volume one (1962) through volume nine (1984), Paul Wasserman was the editor. As is stated under the Editor's Note, it may be best described as a finding guide to statistics. Nearly 4,800 citations are provided under a straight alphabetaical arrangement of subjects. In locating statistics sources on a wide range of topics for materials published in the U.S. or abroad, this is unsurpassable as a guide. Except for the annotated items in "Selected Bibliography of Key Statistical Sources," this set contains only a straight listing of titles.

524. O'Hara, Frederic M., and Sicignano, Robert. *Handbook of United States Economic and Financial Indicators.* Westport, CT: Greenwood Press, 1985. 224 p.

This brings together reference data on the major measures of economic activity in the U.S. The more than 200 measures found here are compiled by some fifty-five sources. It is arranged alphabetically by indicator with cross-references from variant names. Each entry contains a maximum of nine elements including a brief description of the indicator and its use.

525. Powelson, John P., comp. *A Select Bibliography on Economic Development, with Annotations.* Boudler, CO: Westview Press, 1979. 450 p. OCLC 4908125.

This is a bibliography of more than 2,000 titles containing both books and journal articles, primarily those published since 1970. The material is classified according to forty-eight categories. Materials will be found for each major country in Africa, Asia, and Latin America. It does not have an index, but there are cross-references under each topic.

526. Robinson, Judith Schiek. *Subject Guide to US Government Reference Sources.* Littleton, CO: Libraries Unlimited, 1985. 335 p. OCLC 12049806.

This is the revised edition of *Subject Guide to Government Reference Books*, by Sally Wynkoop (1972). This is an annotated guide to over 1,300 reference books seleted for their coverage of the federal government. Economics and related subjects are covered to a considerable extent.

527. Schwarzkopf, LeRoy C., comp. *Government Reference Books; 82/83: A Biennial Guide to US Government Publications.* Littleton, CO: Libraries Unlimited, 1984. 370 p. (Biennial) OCLC 15684706.

This has been published since 1969 and has had three different compilers in addition to the present one. This eighth volume in this series includes 1,191 annotated listings of bibliographies, directories, dictionaries, statistical works, handbooks, almanacs, and other reference sources published by the federal government. The entries are organized by subject under four broad categories: General Library Service; Social Sciences; Science and Technology; and Humanities. These are subdivided into more specific topical and geographical area headings. Economics and related subjects are well represented.

528. Schwarzkopf, LeRoy C. *Guide to Popular US Government Publications.* Litttleton, CO: Libraries Unlimited, 1986. 432 p. OCLC 12943754.

This is a revision of the second edition of *New Guide to Popular Government Publications,* by Walter L. Newsome (1978). The compilation primarily includes publications which have been issued since June 1978. Economics and related subjects figure prominently. Annotations are brief.

529. Sears, Jean L., and Moody, Marilyn K. *Using Government Publications.* Phoenix, AZ: Oryx Press, 1985–86. 2 vols. OCLC 11755915.

The volumes are subtitled as follows: volume one, *Searching Subjects by Agencies*; and volume two, *Finding Statistics and Using Special Techniques.* As stated in the introduction, these volumes provide a basic reference to the use of United States government publications. The set not only lists sources for specific topics but also suggests general and specific strategies for retrieving information. The coverage is extensive and economics and related topics, especially statistics, receive considerable emphasis.

530. Sheehy, Eugene Paul, ed. *Guide to Reference Books.* 10th ed. Chicago: American Library Association, 1986. 1,560 p. OCLC 12103258.

This is a venerable standard guide to general reference works. It has sections on "Economics," and "Statistics and Demography." Selections in these two sections are not as extensive as in *Walford's Guide to Reference Material.*

531. Sichel, Beatrice, and Sichel, Werner, comp. *Economic Journals and Serials: An Analytical Guide.* New York: Greenwood Press, 1986. 285 p.

This bibliography consists of an alphabetical listing of titles with annotations that are both descriptive and evaluative. The scope of the work may be gauzed from the subject headings used in the Classified Title Index at the end of the book. Most of the serial titles listed here are published more than once a year, a few annuals have been included. The book has two indexes, Geographical and Index of Publishers, in addition to the Classified Index mentioned above.

532. *Statistical Reference Index: A Selective Guide to American Statistical Publications from Sources Other Than the US Government.* Washington, DC: Congressional Information Service, 1980–. (Monthly, quarterly, and annual cumulation) OCLC 13072678.

To broaden the coverage of statistical sources, the Congressional Information Service initiated it and patterned it after *American Statistical Index.* This includes statistics published by state governments and private organizations. Subjects covered are economic and social conditions; business; industry; finance; environment; and population.

533. *Subject Guide to Books in Print, 1986–1987.* New York: Bowker, 1986. 4 vols. OCLC 14628961.

This is the thirtieth annual edition of the guide. It is stated that some 625,034 books appear about 786,806 times under 64,891 headings with 54,865 cross-references. It provides subject access to *Books in Print* by subject headings and cross-references that conform to Library of Congress practice. This was produced from the Bibliograhic Information Publication System (BIPS) database of the R.R. Bowker Company. As an offshoot of the BIPS database, a subject selection of entries in the area of economics, industry, finance, management, industrial psychology, vocational guidance, and other business-related topics is available under the title *Business and Economics Books and Serials in Print* beginning with the 1981 edition. The 1973 and 1974 editions were, however, titled *Business Books in Print* and the 1977 edition and its supplement were titled *Business Books and Serials in Print*. The complete *Books in Print* system, called The Books in Print Plus, is available on compact laser disc. Search is possible on the disc in a number of different ways including author, title, subject, language, series title, and publisher.

534. United Nations. Department of International Economic and Social Affairs. *Directory of International Statistics.* New York, 1982. 274 p. OCLC 187676703.
This is volume one, and volume two is yet to be published. This contains a listing of statistical series compiled by the organizations of the U.N. and includes some non-U.N. organizations active in international statistics. The series are listed by subject matter. It also contains an inventory of machine readable databases of economic and social statistics by subject and by organization.

535. United States. Department of Commerce. *Publications Catalogue of the US Department of Commerce.* Washington, DC, 1979–. (Annual) OCLC 7543407.
It is useful for identifying reports and data on a broad range of economic and business topics. It includes publications of the Bureau of the Census, though on a selective basis.

536. United States. Superintendent of Documents. *Monthly Catalogue of US Government Publications.* Washington, DC: U.S. Government Printing Office, 1925 –. OCLC 2264351.
Title varies. This is a monthly publication with semiannual and annual cumulative indexes and a serial supplement. It is the most comprehensive index available for U.S. government publications. Beginning 1976, it changed format, and new elements were introduced in citations which make them comparable to Library of Congress cataloging standards. Indexes include author, title, subject, series, keyword, and Superintendent of Documents (SuDoc) classification number.

537. Verbic, Nada, ed. *Bibliography on Economic Cooperation among Developing Countries, 1981–1982: With Annotations.* Boulder, CO: Westview Press, 1984. 298 p. OCLC 10882233.
This is an international bibliography on economic cooperation and regional integration among developing countries. This covers the period 1981–82 and contains over 2,000 entries of books, articles (from 283 periodicals in nine languages), studies, reports, and official documents, and many of these are annotated. This has been published in association with the Research Centre for Cooperation with Developing Countries (RCCDC), Ljubljana, Yugoslavia. The RCCDC series on South-South

Cooperation each year introduces new studies and reference materials on economic cooperation among developing countries.

538. Walford, Albert J. *Walford's Guide to Reference Material.* London: Library Association, 1980–1987. 3 vols. OCLC 6347136.
The individual volumes are titled as follows: volume one, *Science and Technology* (published 1980); volume two, *Social and Historical Sciences, Philosophy, and Religion* (published 1982); and volume three, *Generalia, Language and Literature, the Arts* (published 1987). This is an extensively annotated list of reference materials containing altogether 20,000 items. It has established itself as an invaluable reference tool for evaluation of references sources and for collection building. It is international in scope, and the focus is, of course, English-language publications. Volume two includes, among other topics, economics, statistics, and commerce. The economics section is quite extensive, running to about seventy pages. It has a combined author, title, and subject index. Volume three, in addition to its own index, contains a combined subject index for all three volumes.

539. Webb, William H. *Sources of Information in the Social Sciences.* 3d ed. Chicago: American Library Association, 1986, 777 p. OCLC 11211042.
This is a standard reference tool, widely used in the social sciences. The section "Economics and Business Administration" gives an extensive coverage of the field. The selections are excellent and the annotations concise and to the point. Each section begins with a survey of the field and then surveys the reference sources, followed by annotations of individual titles, sometimes groups of titles.

540. World Bank. *Index of Publications.* Washignton, DC, 1986. 72 p. (Annual).
This is published every spring and lists all titles in print as of January. It is in four sections. The Titles section provides complete bibliographical information for each title and is in alphabetical order. The Authors section lists authors in alphabetical order with title information only. The Countries and Regions section lists all titles available under specific countries or regions. The Subject Classification section lists all titles available under subject categories. Detailed bibliographical information is not provided under any of the sections other than the title.

541. Wynar, Bohdan S., ed. *American Reference Books Annual, 1987.* Littleton, CO: Libraries Unlimited, 1987. 729 p. OCLC 1028287.
This provides a thorough and critical review of output of reference books. This volume, and the previous ones, has a section on "Economics and Business." The other related sections are "Statistics, Demography, and Urban Studies"; "Transportation"; and "Social Sciences."

542. Wynar, Bohdan S. *Best Reference Books: 1981–1985: Titles of Lasting Value Selected from American Reference Books Annual.* Littleton, CO: Libraries Unlimited, 1986. 504 p. OCLC 13903217.
This provides a selection of over 1,050 refrernce titles determined by the editor to be of lasting value to all types of libraries. These titles were selected from the previous five volumes of *American Reference Books*

Annual. Economics and related fields have been given adequate representation.

543. Zaremba, Joseph. *Statistics and Econometrics: A Guide to Information Sources.* Detroit, MI: Gale Research, 1980. 701 p. OCLC 6863323. This is an annotated bibliography of over 1,700 books. It is in two parts—"Statistics," and "Economics"—and they run into seventeen chapters broken down by subject matter. The coverage is for publications with 1960 or later imprint dates. It has an author, title, and subject index. This is volume fifteen in the Economic Information Guide Series.

Appendix
Developing Countries and Territories
(Arranged in regional groups)

NOTE: There is no universally agreed upon list of developing countries. The one most generally agreed upon is of about 100 countries, and such a list may be found in the *Handbook of World Development* (entry 330). The *Encyclopedia of the Third World* (entry 2) contains a list of 122 countries. U.N. publications (e.g., *UNCTAD Commodity Yearbook*, entry 82) generally list 154 countries as follows:

AFRICA

Eastern Africa

Burundi*
Comoros*
Djibouti*
Ethiopia*
Kenya
Madagascar
Malawi*
Mauritius
Mozambique
Reunion
Rwanda*
Seychelles
Somalia*
Uganda*
United Republic of Tanzania*
Zambia
Zimbabwe

Middle Africa

Angola
Cameroon
Central African Republic*
Chad*
Congo
Equatorial Guinea*
Gabon
Sao Tome and Principe*
Zaire

Northern Africa

Algeria
Egypt
Libyan Arab Jamahiriya

---

* considered least developed country

Morocco
Sudan*
Tunisia

Southern Africa

Botswana*
Lesotho*
Namibia
Swaziland

Western Africa

Benin*
Burkino Faso*
Cape Verde*

Gambia
Ghana
Guinea*
Guinea-Bissau*
Cote d'Ivoire
Liberia
Mali*
Mauritania
Niger*
Nigeria
Saint Helena
Senegal
Sierra Leone*
Togo*

AMERICAS

Caribbean

Antigua and Barbuda
Bahamas
Barbados
British Virgin Islands
Cayman Islands
Cuba
Dominica
Dominican Republic
Grenada
Guadeloupe
Haiti*
Jamaica
Martinique
Monteserrat
Netherlands Antilles
Saint Christopher and Nevis
Saint Lucia
Saint Vincent and the
    Grenadines
Trinidad and Tobago
Turks and Caicos Islands
United States Virgin Islands

Central America

Belize
Costa Rica
El Salvador
Guatemala
Honduras
Mexico
Nicaragua
Panama

North America

Bermuda
Greenland
St. Pierre and Miquelon

South America

Argentina
Bolivia
Brazil
Chile
Colombia
Ecuador
Falkland Islands (Maldinas)
French Guyana

Guyana
Paraguay
Peru

Suriname
Uruguay
Venezuela

ASIA

Eastern Asia

China
Hong Kong
Korea (Dem. People's Rep.)
Macau
Mongolia

Indonesia
Lao People's Dem. Rep.*
Malaysia
Philippines
Singapore
Thailand
Viet Nam

South Asia

Afghanistan*
Bangladesh*
Bhutan
India
Iran
Maldives*
Nepal*
Pakistan
Sri Lanka

Western Asia

Bahrain
Cyprus
Democratic Yemen*
Iraq
Jordan
Kuwait
Lebanon
Oman
Qatar
Saudi Arabia
Syrian Arab Republic
Turkey
United Arab Emirates
Yemen

Southeastern Asia

Brunei Darussalam
Burma
Democratic Kampuchea

EUROPE

Malta

Yugoslavia

OCEANIA

American Samoa
Cook Islands
Fiji
French Polynesia

Guam
Kiribati
Nauru
New Caledonia

Niue
Pacific Islands
Papua New Guinea
Samoa
Solomon Islands
Tokelau

Tonga
Tuvalu
Vanuatu*
Wake Island
Wallis and Futuna Islands

Author Index

Numbers refer to citation numbers, not to page numbers.

Title Index

Numbers refer to citation numbers, not to page numbers.

Subject Index

Numbers refer to citation numbers, not to page numbers.